MW01616901

What's age got to do with it?

Living life and defying the myths of aging, 83 year old Joan Kennedy, motivational speaker, seminar leader and entrepreneur has spent a lifetime battling lfe's adversitites with humor, grit and joy. She has spread her philosophy with books and speaking engagements across the country. Three major factors in living the good life with zest and productivity are simply "don't buy into the myths of aging," building a health self-esteem and keep having dreams and setting goals for the future.

For those who view themselves as "has beens," help is available and entertaining. The source of this dash of wit and wisdom, Joan has spent over 25 years striding across stages with the zest of a thirty year old, proudly billing herself as the "oldest female motivational speaker in the country."

Speaking of self-confidence, how many of us are enthusiastically announcing our age on stages across the country? An ex-model, she still looks great but more importantly, it's the total joy of life that is obvious before she picks up the microphone. She gives the impression of being able to "outrun, outshoot" anyone else. She is unstoppable! And she does it with sparkling dialogue and effervescence.

Also by Joan Kennedy

I Don't Want Much From Life, I Want More

How To Keep Your Staying Power

Everybody's Doing It

Lull-A-Baby (Musical CD)

What's age got to do with it?

By

Joan Kennedy

Younique Press

© 2005 All rights reserved. No part of this book may be reproduced in any form whatsoever, by photography or xerography or by any other means, by broadcast or transmission, by translation into any kind of language, nor by recording electronically or otherwise, except by a reviewer, who may quote brief passages in critical articles or reviews.

Cover Design: Laura E. Davies
Cover Photo Credit: Ghislain & Marie David de Lossy
Book Format: Accurate Press, Inc.

ISBN: 0-9601920-4-2

For my children, Bob, Marnie, Patty and Amy,
who brought so much love,
joy and humor to my life.

Foreword

In his book, *Live a Thousand Years*, Giovanni Livera reminds us to measure the quality of our life by moments and memories, rather than clocks and calendars.

When I think of Joan Kennedy and the wisdom and insights she shares in this book, it takes me back to our first meeting in December of 1982. I was twenty-one years old, and Joan introduced me to the world of professional speaking, and the National Speakers Association. My life and career have never been the same.

But it was her boundless enthusiasm and unwavering belief in me that captivated my heart, and we became instant friends. She believes in you too. Otherwise, she would not have written this book.

Joan is one of those rare people who say, "Why not?" to the world, when others simply question, "Why should I?" and go about their lives in an endless search for satisfaction and fulfillment.

You will delight in her "make a garden" story and feel her loss in the fire that devastated her spirit. I was fortunate enough to be with her during that difficult time, to listen to her and watch her spring from the ashes. You will be inspired by her strength and courage in creating a whole new and exciting chapter in her life.

What's age got to do with it? is sure to be a book you will read more than once. The insights and strategies she shares will help you get more of anything you want in your life. I also hope you get to hear her speak one day, and to meet her. Your life will never be the same either.

– Mark LeBlanc, Author of *Growing Your Business*

Acknowledgments

So many people have been with me on this journey. From writing this book, I learned that I could not have done it alone.

I would like to extend my deepest thanks and appreciation to a number of people who made a special contribution with their ideas and insights. Thank you, Ellajane Knott for encouraging me to write this book.

My very special thanks to my daughter, Marnie, for all your help, offering suggestions and giving me the encouragement I needed from time to time.

A special thanks to Freddie Motta, my son-in-law, whose computer skills helped me prepare this manuscript. Thank you for taking the time out of your busy schedule to help me.

Donna Guenk, who although involved in a number of community works, still found the time to review my manuscript and give me some excellent suggestions

To Pam Lund for your editing, enthusiasm and personal involvement in this project. My special thanks to you.

To Connie Anderson, the final editor who gave this book a delightful added character by her suggestions, handholding and enthusiasm for the content. She was also involved in composing the text for the back cover.

To Andrea Pike, who I want to thank for her willingness to share an idea that added a great dimension to the book.

My thanks to Denise Herbst, who handled all the final details of the manuscript and I watched as she gave life and breath to this book in her professional, efficient and joyous manner.

My thanks to Lee Boyan, Caroline Branstad, Beverly Harris, Judi Milton, Elizabeth Rheinhardt, Paulette Salo, Elaine Stindt, Penny Swartz, Mary Walberg and Arlene Williams, for sharing some of your life-journey experiences.

Table of Contents

Chapter 1

"How old would you be,
if you didn't know how old you was?"

– Satchel Page

How Old is Old?

When I was 65 years old, I lost everything in a house fire. One day I was in business; the next day, I wasn't. Overnight, fifteen years of work was gone; the books I had written, the tapes I created, my speaking and promotional material, files and contact information.   My desk, with everything on, under and in it, was destroyed.

As far as I was concerned, my life as a speaker was over. As devastating as that was, however, the worst was yet to come. For the first time in my life, I felt old, empty and without purpose. Before the fire, I was too busy to think about the fact that I was 65. Afterwards, all the myths I had previously scoffed at about being 65, came back to haunt me. "You're old at 65." "It's time to quit." "You're finished." Now they had new meaning for me.

In the days and nights that followed, as I sat in a rented apartment with rented furniture and no personal possessions, I focused on all the negative aspects of aging. I had a problem accepting that anything good was associated with this time in my life.

As my house was being rebuilt, I started reading books on aging. I wanted to find out if there was anything positive to look forward to. One day while reading the monthly AARP magazine, I came across the following statistic: "the fastest-growing age group in this country are people in their 80s." Eighties! Here I was only 65. I could have fifteen or twenty more productive years ahead of me. It suddenly seemed unthinkable that I should waste another moment lamenting my age. There was time – plenty of time – to start over.

The thought that I could begin anew sustained me during the following weeks and months. At times the task of putting the pieces together again was so overwhelming I wanted to chuck it all. It soon became clear to me that if I was to make it, I had to stay focused. I had to move forward, one day at a time, and not give up. It took me two years to put my house back in order and to re-organize my speaking business.

Based on my own experiences, I realized that in a longer life we have second and third chances and opportunities to begin again, *but only if we believe that growing old is a state of mind.*

Today many people are apprehensive about aging, becasue it will mean the loss of youth, health, status, sttractiveness and personal effectiveness. With images like this, it's no wonder so many have come to dislike and fear the aging process and to expect the worst. Dr. Walter Bortz, author of *Living Longer for Dummies*, says, "Aging is a self-fulfilling prophecy."

Aging Doesn't Mean It's Over

The fact is that in our global population of six billion people, one person in 10 is over 60. In the year 2006, the first of the baby boomers will turn 60 – which means four million a year like them.

Everyday is the beginning of something new – no matter how old you are. And in this day and age, it's becoming harder and harder to say for certain how old one has to be to be old. Unfortunately, a great number of people continue to accept the archaic ideas of aging, and consequently create for themselves a negative image of their own aging.

I overheard two early-50's women in a restaurant talking about aging. One woman said, "It's tough to get old. Everything falls apart or slows down." The other woman commented, "My mother always says: Wait, it gets worse."

Unfortunately, society's image of the "older woman' has not quite caught up with reality. We are still burdened by a lack of positive role models in advertising, film and television.

Since the way we feel about ourselves has a great deal to do with our self-image, we need to take stock of ourselves. To begin with, we were never entirely satisfied with the way we looked, even as teenagers. Now we have to contend with gray thinning hair   fine lines and wrinkles, age spots on many parts of the body. Then there is gravity to deal with. A reporter once asked Gypsy Rose Lee, the famous strip tease artist how she felt about being forty. She said, I feel great about it. I have everything I had when I was twenty, it's just lower."

One of the first things we can lose as we grow older is our self-image. This is not apparent when we look in the mirror. With the loss of this quality, we don't feel as good about ourselves as we once did.

After the fire, I had an experience that made me aware of how fragile one's self-image can be. Before the fire, I was busy, confident and goal-oriented. After the fire, it seemed, my only goal was to be safe.

On the morning of the fire, I rushed out of the house in my flannel nightgown and a pair of wool socks. The only thing I grabbed, were the keys to my car. I always kept them on a hook next to the back door.

The question has been asked many times, "What would you take out of your house if it was on fire?" Many people will say, "photographs." Photographs did not enter my mind, neither did underwear, shoes, purse or my winter coat, even though it was the 27th of January.

I drove to my daughter's home, which was near by. She gave me my grandson's black loafers, my son-in-law's royal blue leisure suit, a leather purse and a white fake fur coat. After I got dressed, I looked like I lived under a bridge.

That morning a woman, from the Red Cross, came to my daughter's home and gave me a reservation for three days at the Day's Inn, and a $50.00 voucher to buy clothes at a department store near the motel.

The same day of the fire, I thought I'd shop for a pair of shoes. As I entered the department store, I saw a large sign, 'Tennis Shoes $9.95.' I knew immediately I had my first purchase, with money left over. A young man approached me, and I told him I'd like to try on the tennis shoes for

$9.95. He brought the tennis shoes to me. I tried them on and they fit. I said, "I'll take them." As we walked to the register, he said, "Will that be cash or charge?" I said, "Well, not exactly," and with that, I handed the voucher to him. He looked at it and said, "What is this?" I tried to explain why I had it and what it was for, but he totally ignored me. He said, "I don't know what this is, and I have other customers to wait on." He handed the voucher back to me and walked away, leaving me standing at the register. I walked out of the department store that evening embarrassed, humiliated and without my tennis shoes.

After that incident, I vowed that I would never allow anyone ever again to make me feel unimportant, obsolete or invisible. In retrospect, I should have demanded to see the manager and to tell him or her about my predicament. I am sure that I would have walked out of the store that evening, with my new tennis shoes and a feeling of well being. When Dr. Robert Butler, president and CEO of the International Longevity Center, was asked whether he recommended growing old gracefully, he replied, "I don't think that's the way to go – being sweet and nice, not making noise. I would recommend growing old candidly, open-mindedly and with flexibility."

Are Your Beliefs Aging You?

The negative myths that society holds about people past the age of 55 is that they lose their vitality, creativity and personal effectiveness. If we accept the fact that 60, 70 or 80 is old, then we accept the fact that we have reached an age where we can no longer grow. We have to assume that what we have achieved is all that we can hope to achieve, and from now on, it's all down hill.

This concept is reinforced every day in our media. In product advertising for aging that run the gamut from menopause to Medicare and everything in between. We have learned in a hundred ways to revere what is young and dislike what is old. We focus on the negative aspects of aging and seem to have a problem accepting that it has lots of good associated with it, too. In our culture focused on youth, we've been forced to see each birthday, after 55, as a harbinger of the lost youth, vitality, attractiveness, strength and sexuality.

In 1934 the U.S. Social Security system was signed into law. As a result, people accepted the belief that the calendar now tells us when we are old. It tells us when we lose our ability to function successfully in the business world.

It's up to us to take a realistic view of ourselves, to determine the opportunities that are ahead of us in our future. To consider what action we need to take to ensure that our future will be productive, fulfilling and satisfying.

While our ideas about aging are changing, there is a belief among an overwhelming number of people that when you are sixty or over, you become more rigid, rather than adaptable to change. The negative images we harbor, of our later years, have a tremendously destructive influence on us.

When I started writing this book, I asked a wide range of ages, "How do you feel about getting older?" Here are some of the negative comments I received:

"Society does not value anyone over 55."
"People over 60 are no longer productive."
"When you're 60, you're old."
"Most older men and women are in poor health."
"Older people are less attractive and less valued.
"Anyone over 55 is shelf material."
"After 60, you're no longer in the mainstream."
"It's too late after 60 to make any significant changes."
"After 60; there's no time left for new ventures;
    it's just easier to stay with the status quo."
"When you're over 60, you don't have romance,
    you're not as mobile, and sex is a thing of the past."

Dr. Gayle Olinekova, who wrote the book *Power Aging*, reminds us that "Everything changes based on how we perceive it. If you want to believe that aging is terrible and that you are doomed to live your life in misery and depression, then you will not be disappointed."

It's now time for all of us, whatever our age, to take a long, hard look at the beliefs we hold that reflect a less-than-positive view of the aging process. If we are to create a more positive image, we need to dispel the myths and stereotypes that bind us. We need to listen to our own body, mind and instincts, and not to what our neighbors or friends may think and say. There are enough facts to deal with regarding the aging process. Let's not muddy the waters with myths.

The Good News

In the past, the emphasis was on youth. Today, the emphasis is on aging. We can't pick up a newspaper or a magazine, turn on the radio or television without reading, hearing or seeing something about aging. This is because of the aging of the baby boomers, who have been turning 50 at the rate of four million a year – seven every minute. In the year 2006 the first of the baby boomers will start turning sixty.

Lydia Bronte, Ph.D., who wrote *The Longevity Factor*, said, "You may find that your adult life will be twice as long as you think it is going to be. If you have had reasonably good health habits, by the time you celebrate your sixtieth birthday, instead of being on the downward slope of old age, you may have two or three decades of productive adult time ahead of you." If you are not aware of this trend, you may make decisions that essentially foreshorten your own opportunities. You could reach sixty and think your most creative and productive years are behind you.

According to the Census Bureau, for example, the United States has over 50,000 people who are 100 years old or older. By the year 2020, it is estimated that there will be over 266,000 people who will reach the age of 100.

Many believe that living longer only means that we'll spend much more time being old. Lucky for us, what is really happening is that the physical process of aging has gradually been slowed down. We are not only living longer, we are entering old age later in life. The only sane decision we can make is to take a positive view of our own aging.

It's also important to keep in mind that there is always room for creative thought, new options and new discoveries as long as we live. No one should drop out of life at any time. In fact, as long as we live, there isn't a set date or line in the sand that says, "We're finished."

It is up to us to take a realistic view of ourselves, to consider what we need to do to ensure that our future will be productive, fulfilling and satisfying. Life holds no real success until we find that which fulfills us. We lose time not finding it and each birthday only serves as a reminder of lost opportunities.

How to Keep Your Staying Power

Life is dynamic, never static. We are always in the process of growth. As the years pass, we do lose specific roles and responsibilities. We are finished with certain stages of our lives. But as human beings, we are never finished. Nothing could be more destructive to the human spirit than the idea that there are no more dreams, no more challenges, no more new exciting experiences.

Caroline Branstad is in her 80s and drives a pink Pontiac Grand Prix. When her husband died at age forty-seven, Caroline needed to find a way to earn a living. In 1975 she began working as a Mary Kay consultant.

Today, she is an Independent Senior Sales Director, overseeing consultants from around the country, in states such as New Mexico, Maine, Minnesota and Wisconsin. Though she is semi-retired, Caroline still makes a fair number of sales calls herself to customers she has accumulated over the years. During her time with the company, she has been rewarded with twelve cars (two of them were pink Cadillacs). She has no plans to retire. In fact, she says, "I love what I do. I have the opportunity to meet some wonderful, exciting people through my work."

"One of the important things I have found," she says, "is that, as long as you live, you can learn new skills, engage in new kinds of work, meet new people, and have new relationships."

You Are Your Own Main Event

One of the most important factors in successful aging, and a quality we begin to lose as we age, is self-confidence. It is the ingredient that results in self-assurance and the conviction that we can deal successfully with life and its challenges. When we are confident, we have a deep inner belief in our self-worth, in our abilities and in our importance as a human being.

Projecting confidence is a result of being in control of the messages we send. People don't know otherwise unless we send signals that tell them we are not sure of ourselves. Eye contact, the way we walk, and our posture often communicate these signals.

One way to gain self-confidence is to practice these simple techniques:

- Make sure you have good eye contact when you are talking, as well as listening to others.
- Make everything about you say, "I'm confident."

- Don't show hesitation when you walk into a room filled with strangers.
- When walking anywhere, look as though you are going some place important.
- Speak up.
- Smile big.

Confident living can begin when we realize that life is a process of continual change, and it can always be changed for the better. It also comes from knowing who we are and what is possible.

Mary Walberg is a wife, mother and married to a prominent man in their community. "However," she said, "I felt like a non-entity." So, when their children were grown and educated, she decided at forty-seven to go back to school and become a nurse.

She said, "I would advise anyone who feels down, to get going. Get out, and do something for themselves if they have the health to do so." She said, "I have one regret, I should have done it sooner."

No one else is going to come along to make your life more than it is. Your life is an individual responsibility, an individual opportunity and an individual experience.

In his book, *From the Summit of Years Four Score*, Samuel Ullman wrote: "You are as young as your faith, as old as your doubt; as young as your confidence, as old as your fear; as young as your hope, as old as your despair."

This is a short list of things to do to stay in the action and to be a part of the scene:

- Stay positive.
- Preserve what you've got.
- Stay close to family and friends.
- Exercise every day to keep fit.
- Eat well to stay healthy.
- Stay involved in life and with people.
- Find your passion.
- Live in the present, plan for the future.

Life is too short, too wonderful to live it in mediocrity. Continue to develop all aspects of yourself: mental, physical and spiritual. As Helen Keller once said, "Life is either a great adventure, or it's nothing."

In looking ahead to the years after 60, we can begin to see the potential for great achievement. Recent studies show that a person is capable of functioning beautifully, not only productively and creatively, but also intellectually and sexually, well into their 80s and beyond. Betty Friedan, author of *The Feminine Mystique* and *The Fountain of Age*, said "Aging is not lost youth but a new stage of opportunity and strength."

It is important to look to the future with purpose, power, possibilities and a sense of adventure. A longer life gives us second and third chances to go back and do some of the things we weren't able to do earlier in life.

In the final analysis, the antidote for aging is action, both mental and physical. So whatever dreams you once had for yourself, bring them back. They may be even more exciting the second time around.

It's Your Move

Write your thoughts on each of these questions.

• What have I always wanted?

_____

_____

_____

• What have I always wanted to do?

_____

_____

_____

• What have I always wanted to be good at?

_____

_____

_____

• What have I always wanted to do with my family?

_____

_____

_____

- What have I always wanted to do with my friends?

_____

_____

_____

- What have I always wanted to learn?

_____

_____

_____

- What do I want to experience?

_____

_____

_____

- What do I want to change?

_____

_____

_____

The medical profession is proving that a person's mental and physical health is greatly affected to the degree that a person has found specific life purposes. So keep on digging up those old dreams: "I always want to…" "I always dreamed of being… ." To begin, work on some variation of any dream you have wanted to pursue. "Use what you have to run toward your best," said Oprah Winfrey.

Remember, whether you are 55, 65 or 85, everybody's doing it…growing older. For those willing to plan their own adventures and create their own joy, life has more to offer.

Just to Remind You...

To understand why we feel what we feel about aging, we have to dispel or rethink long-held myths and stereotypes.

- No one knows for certain how old one has to be to be old.

- If you are to create a more positive image of your own aging, you need to dispel the myths and stereotypes that bind you.

- As long as you live, there isn't a set date or line in the sand that says, "you're finished."

- It's now time for you, whatever your age, to take a long, hard look at the beliefs you hold that reflect a less-than-positive view of your own aging.

- There are enough facts to deal with regarding the aging process. Let's not muddy the waters with myths.

- In the past, the emphasis was on youth. Today, the emphasis is on aging.

- Everything about aging is based on how you perceive it.

- It is important to keep in mind that there is always room for creative thought, new options and new discoveries as long as you live.

- Life holds no real success until you find that which fulfills you.

- As long as you live, you can learn new skills, engage in new kinds of work, meet new people, and have new relationships.

- A longer life gives us second and third chances to go back and do some of the things we weren't able to do earlier in life.

- It is important to have a deep inner belief in your self-worth, in your abilities and in your importance as a human being.

- It is up to you to take a realistic view of yourself, to consider what you need to do to ensure that your future will be productive, fulfilling and satisfying.

- It is important to look to the future with purpose, power, possibilities and a sense of adventure.

- Life is too short, too wonderful to live it in mediocrity. Continue to develop all aspects of yourself, mental, physical and spiritual.

Chapter 2

"Do what you like.
It can help you look healthier and younger.
You are never too old to develop new interests.
Take a gamble and jump into a new project."

— Dr. Sarah Peyton, 83

Avoid the Ruts

At any age, we should all have a smorgasbord of enjoyable experiences – of love, work, friendship, hobbies, travel and any other area that needs awakening. Yet occasionally, almost everyone slips into a comfortable and often boring track. When we're in a rut, we fail to update the ways we think and live. If we are no longer learning from new experiences or growing as a person, it means we are missing out on a big part of life.

As creatures of habit, many of us follow the path of least resistance. It's so much easier to awaken each day, at a given time, and look forward to a day of routine and schedules than to awaken earlier and do something different. Although we may want to go another way, we allow ourselves to follow the old joyless path because it's just a lot easier. There are those of us who feel safe and secure in familiar surroundings, doing familiar things with familiar people.

Gerontologists agree that human beings must remain

active at the cost of stagnation; that the elixir of life is mental activity. We need to avoid ruts, fixed habits and old ways.

But of course, before you can even begin to climb out of a rut, you need to be aware that you are in one. Boredom is the first sign. If it feels like the same old, same old, it probably is. When you retire at night and think back over your day, you have to ask yourself, "Was there anything different or new about today, or was it pretty much like yesterday?" If it was, it's time to do something about it. After all, it's your life.

True, there are conditions in our lives that we can't control, and there are physical, financial and social limits to what we can do at any given period. But there is no doubt that the most powerful limits are the "inner limits" we impose on ourselves as we grow older.

Confront Rather Than Complain

Years ago, I kept complaining to a friend about a bothersome situation I could have remedied. She said to me, "Joan, fish or cut bait." The remark was blunt, but true.

At some time in our lives, many of us may come to a point when we finally say, "That's it, I have had it with my job...a relationship...lack of money." At that point we're ready to make a change. Yet, when that happens we tend to sputter, complain and wait until the feeling passes and things return to normal.

Elizabeth Rheinhardt is a happily married woman today, with two wonderful children. But, she said, "It hasn't always been that way. In my marriage, I had everything to be happy about, but it just didn't seem like enough. Before I had children, I was a very confident hairdresser. I loved doing things for people. It was fun doing something creative and making others look good at the same time."

"After the children," she said, "I became a bore. I was totally dependent on my husband for everything. I knew inside of me somewhere there was that other independent, confident person. And I just wanted to get her out."

Elizabeth felt that a confident, well-established man like her husband would never understand her feelings, and those who did, like her friends, were either afraid to admit that they felt the same way, or couldn't help anyway.

She had a part-time job, but it was uninteresting. Her bosses were all younger than she was. She said, "They acted as if they were the knowledgeable superiors. I didn't begrudge them their position, but at thirty-five years of age, I felt I was back down to the position I was in when I was sixteen."

Aside from working part-time, she said, "I cooked, cleaned the house, took care of the children and did some of her husband's paperwork. It just seemed to me like a thankless merry-go-round."

Then one day, she and her mother were on their way to visit her sister. It wasn't long before Elizabeth started complaining about her life again. Her mother stopped her in mid-sentence and said, "You must enjoy being a martyr!" Elizabeth said, "Her words really stung."

Her mother went on to say, "You've been wallowing in self-pity for so many years. I'm tired of listening to you and so are a lot of other people. Stop complaining and do something about your situation."

Elizabeth said, "My mother never talked to me like that before. In the past, she just listened to me." That outburst really affected her. She said, "It was difficult to get my mother's words out of my thoughts. It didn't take long to realize that I either had to stop complaining about my life or do something about it." She said, "I love my husband and children, but I knew that I had to satisfy my own personal needs."

Elizabeth started making plans to go back to work. "To begin with, I had to find the time to do what I wanted to do and to make time for all my responsibilities. I started with a list of all the things I did from morning until night. The list covered my daily routine. First I eliminated all of the non-productive things I did on a daily basis, like the habit of spending time on the phone each morning complaining to my friends."

Elizabeth then set priorities for each day so that she wouldn't get bogged down in activities that had little importance. She said, "I also brought my husband and children into my plans. I found that as I assumed more control over my life, I became more efficient."

"The best thing is I have more confidence in myself again. I am now a beauty operator with many clients." Elizabeth still gives credit to her mother. She said, "It took a lot of strength for mother to talk to me as she did. I thank her for that."

We use up tremendous energy rebelling against situations we do nothing about, whether it is a relationship, life in general, or dissatisfaction with the way we look.

If we are unhappy with ourselves or the way our life is going, we need to do something about it. Nothing happens until we make a decision to change.

Is there something you are doing that you do not enjoy? How could you eliminate that activity? Is it possible to stop doing it? Is there someone else who could be doing it for you? Dare to drop one thing from your routine this week.

What Is This Thing Called Happiness?

The easiest thing in the world to accomplish is unhappiness. If we go around telling ourselves and others things are not going well, nothing is satisfactory, things in our lives are not going to change (except perhaps get worse), we can be sure of the outcome. It takes a certain amount of discipline to stay happy.

None of us was born unhappy. We were not born with a negative self-image. We were not born with self-destructive habits. We were not born with the fear of failure. All of the things that limit us and make us unhappy, we have learned through the years. If we are not happy most of the time, one thing we can do is to improve our outlook.

While there are no quick fixes in improving your outlook, the greatest indicator of general life satisfaction is simply satisfaction with self. Studies show that the people who think well of themselves are less vulnerable to life's inevitable setbacks and struggles. These studies underscore the power of a healthy self-esteem.

Chances are if you like the person you see in the mirror every morning, you'll be happier and feel good about yourself. One study done by the University of Michigan showed that the 15 percent who felt in control of their lives and satisfied with themselves had "extraordinary" positive feelings of happiness.

Other studies show the importance of humor. People who enjoy life and are happy tend to have less sickness and stress than people who take life very seriously and resist seeing life's lighter side.

Entertainer/comedian Victor Borge said, "Laughter is the shortest distance between two people." Everyone likes to be around people with a good sense of humor, who laugh easily. When we are laughing, it is impossible to feel unhappy.

Getting Unstuck

Certain general principles apply in breaking out of a rut, no matter why we seem to be stuck. We need to take responsibility for our own lives. We need to stop making statements such as, "I don't have the time or energy," or "I'm just too old." If we complain that we're unable to do anything about our circumstances, we need to take another look. Ask yourself:

- What did I enjoy doing five years ago that I no longer do?
- Why did I stop?
- What would it take to start doing it again?

Often dissatisfaction is the push we need to change. The pull is the pleasure and accomplishment that follows. We need new experiences, new settings and new relationships.

When we break free of confining habits, we acquire a wide range of benefits. Our minds think in new ways, we become more energetic and more creative, and the overall effect is that we are happier. Best of all, the process can begin with small steps.

Here are few things that can be done to keep mentally and physically active and to avoid ruts, fixed habits and old ways:

- Stay enthusiastic about life.
- Learn new skills: a new language, book binding, improving your computer skills, or any other activity that appeals to you.
- Pursue stimulating activities such as reading, traveling and attending cultural events.
- Do crossword puzzles and other mind-challenging games.
- Engage in physical activities such as walking, swimming, biking and workouts at the gym.
- Stay socially active: Join a book club, attend the theater or museums with friends, form a birthday lunch club, and find ways to mix with people.
- Be flexible and adaptable, rather than always doing things the same old way.

Enthusiasm Creates Excitement

Whether we're aware of it, we're all capable of showing enthusiasm. Enthusiasm will not only keep us feeling young and vital, it is the necessary ingredient for success. Ralph Waldo Emerson said, "Nothing great was ever achieved without enthusiasm."

The opposite of enthusiasm is apathy. Sometimes we insist on looking for problems. We feel the rainy day is bound to come, and we do our best to make it happen, preparing for and fearing it. We cross our bridges a hundred times before we come to them.

The way we begin our day sets the tone. We condition ourselves in the first few moments of awareness. We always have a choice. We can think discouraging thoughts that can be depressing, or positive thoughts that fill us with enthusiasm. Each day's choice will determine the quality of our life.

So, instead of thinking about all the gloomy things that could happen, we need to think of all the good things we have, such as family, friends, a healthy body, a powerful mind, and yes, the wonderment of another day. And during the day, enthusiasm or the lack of it will show through everything we do. It doesn't take much effort to be an enthusiastic person. Your behavior will echo or demonstrate or reinforce the power of your enthusiasm.

- When you shake hands with someone, make your hand clasp say, "I'm glad to know you." No hand shake at all is better than a limp handshake.

- Put life into your smile. People will see a warm, enthusiastic personality, someone they like to be around. When you are talking to family or friends, tell them your good news for the day.

- Be an "I feel great person." When you meet some one and they ask you how you are, don't tell them about your aches and pains. People really don't want to hear about them. The question, "How are you?" is only a salutation, not an opening for a health report. At every possible opportunity, say, "I feel great."

An enthusiastic person is invariably more interesting to be around. We gain nothing by appearing blasé or by whining. If we give the impression that we don't care what is going on around us, then others are likely to find our apathy unappealing.

Change Is Good for the Soul

We need change, even if it is only for the sake of change. A change of scene, a change of what we read, eat or drink, what we wear, a new hobby, all can jar us back to the realization that no matter how long we have lived, there is always something new and interesting that we have not done or experienced. Consider the words of Henry Van Dyke, "Be glad of life because it gives you the chance to love and to work and to play and to look at the stars."

Then let your instincts lead you naturally to that which

excites you and makes you feel good about yourself and your life.

It's Your Move
Write your thoughts on each of these questions.

• Why do you think people like to be around enthusiastic people?

_____

_____

_____

• Why is enthusiasm such an important quality to possess?

_____

_____

_____

• How do you feel about people who never seem to get excited about anything?

_____

_____

_____

No matter where you live, whether it's a large city or a small town, you can do well if you keep learning, growing and motivating yourself to move ahead, rather than remaining stuck in old routines. Anthropologist Ashley Montagu, Ph.D., writes in her book, *Growing Young,* "We are designed to learn and explore all our lives."

Remember, no one can assume responsibility for your life. If you are dissatisfied or bored with it, it's up to you to do something about it.

Just to Remind You...

When we're in a rut, we fail to update the way we think and live our lives, we're no longer learning, and now follow in the path of least resistance.

- Your life should have a smorgasbord of enjoyable experiences, of love, work, friendship, hobbies, travel and any other area that needs awakening.

- Boredom is the first sign we're in a rut.

- "Was there anything different or new about today, or was it pretty much like yesterday?" If it was, it's time to do something about it. After all, it's your life.

- Fish or cut bait! Confront rather than complain. Figure out what you want and do it!

- Set priorities. Eliminate non-productive things from your life to help find the time to do what is really important to you.

- We were NOT born unhappy. The easiest thing in the world to accomplish is unhappiness. All the things that limit us and make us unhappy we have learned through the years.

- The greatest indicator of general satisfaction is simply satisfaction with self.

- Enthusiasm will not only keep you feeling young and vital, it is the necessary ingredient for success.

- We cross our bridges a hundred times before we come to them.

- Let your instincts lead you naturally to that which excites you and makes you feel good about yourself and your life.

- Each day's choices will determine the quality of your life.

When you break free of confining habits, you acquire a wide range of benefits. Your mind thinks in new ways, you become more energetic and more creative, and the overall affect is that you're *happier*.

Chapter 3

*"Something we were withholding made us weak
until we found it was ourselves."*

– Robert Frost, American Poet

Restore a Strong Inner Belief

For years my married life had fluctuated between feelings of frustration and contentment. When I was frustrated, I took down walls, moved furniture and changed my kitchen curtains. When I was content, I vacuumed, dusted and baked bread.

During the years when I was married and raising my children, I realized I was forever busy. The decorating, remodeling and all my other busy work were an escape. I was avoiding the real conflicts within my life and myself. My marriage was crumbling. I had no future in terms of marketable skills. I was forty-five, with three children at home, very little work experiences and no money of my own.

During the years I was married, I was never concerned with looking for a job or preparing myself for one, either mentally or emotionally. I had no expectations of working outside of my home. I saw no need for any further planning. I thought I had achieved my major goal in life, the role of wife and mother. I didn't want to make any drastic changes.

A feeling of panic would set in each time I considered giving up my familiar ways and accepting the challenge of the unknown. The thought of undertaking anything as monumental as getting a job was frightening.

After many financial setbacks, I finally decided to find a job. With my sketchy work experience, the thoughts that kept surfacing were, "What can I possibly do?" and "Who'd want me?" The business world was not holding its breath for my potential contribution. It was clear to me no one would hire me because I was just a housewife. Many times I asked myself, "How could I have spent so many years on this earth and not ended up with something I could do to make a living?"

Prior to my marriage, I had worked in a factory on an assembly line; then as a receptionist in an office; and finally as a model for a department store. The thought of going back to factory work depressed me, and I discounted the possibility of getting a job in fashion because I was just too old. I was wearing my skirts two inches below my knees and the stores were selling theirs four inches above (and higher). It was a foregone conclusion that the world of fashion was the last place I would try to look.

At the suggestion of a friend, I applied for a job at the University of Minnesota. Along with my application, I was told I had to take a Civil Service test. Before the test began, I filled out a number of forms about my education and work experiences. After completing all the required questions, I started the second phase of the test that included math problems, word association, finger dexterity and others I have blocked from my consciousness in the ensuing years. When

I finally completed the tests, I was told to wait in the corridor for the results.

Some time passed, and finally the personnel manager came out of an office and walked over to me. He didn't take me into his office, he just stood in the hallway and said, "Mrs. Kennedy, you passed the tests, but you don't know how to do anything." Well, I knew that before I left home in the morning. Now he knows it and everyone in earshot knows that I don't know how to do anything!

I don't remember my answer, if any. All I remember is the embarrassment I felt. Then he said, "We do have a part-time job at Nicholson Hall Bookstore." Although the job was only two weeks out of each quarter, I jumped at the opportunity. I finally had a job!

My enthusiasm diminished when I realized the bookstore would provide no challenge or training or even adequate income. For the extra money I needed, I worked for my friends. I painted, refinished furniture, mended Oriental rugs, ironed and cleaned houses.

Self-Image: The Bottom Line

At the time, I didn't know how to do any better, so I just carried on. An old Chinese saying, "When the student is ready, the teacher will appear." My teacher came in the form of a book, and it changed the course of my life. I read a book review on *Psycho Cybernetics* by Maxwell Maltz, M.D. Although I didn't have a clue what the title meant, I continued to read. One line caught my eye. It said, very simply, "Chances are, if life has passed you by, it's because you yourself have not unlatched your success door." Well, I knew I had to read the book. I picked it up at the library and began. I knew immediately *Psycho Cybernetics* was a book I had to own.

As I began to read its theories and philosophy, everything started to make sense. "Whether you realize it or not, on a conscious level," Maxwell Maltz said, "you have within yourself a mental picture of the kind of person you think you are. All your actions, feelings, behavior, even your abilities are always consistent with this image. In short, you will 'act like' the sort of person you conceive yourself to be." Once I had read the book, I realized I had set up my own limitations in my mind, and that's where I had to make the changes.

Months later, after re-reading the book several times and following the techniques laid out, I asked myself again, "What can I do?" "What skills do I have?" "What talents do I have to offer?" This time, when my experiences as a model surfaced in my mind, instead of thinking, "Who'd want me?" something had changed. I felt differently about myself. I could truthfully say, "Why not me? I have the talent." It didn't seem ridiculous to try to get back into the fashion business. For the first time, I knew in my heart I could do it.

I called to schedule an interview at one of the leading department stores and was given an appointment for the following month. From that point until the day of the interview, I visualized the interview. I went over in my mind all the various questions the fashion director would likely ask me and thought about the answers I would give.

Maxwell Maltz also writes about the power of our imagination. He said that, "Mental pictures offer us an opportunity to practice new traits and attitudes, which otherwise we could not do. This is possible because your nervous system cannot tell the difference between an actual experience and one that is vividly imagined."

Each night after I got into bed I would completely relax. Then I rehearsed the interview in my mind. Every night, as I pictured the interview, I heard the fashion director saying, "You're hired."

One month later, armed with a feeling of great expectations, a new self-image, and a two-piece dress exposing my knees for the first time in more than twenty years, I felt especially confident as I headed for my fashion interview. We were not too far along when the interviewer told me she was losing her fashion assistant, who was pregnant. She went on to say that she had made up her mind that the next fashion assistant would be a mature woman who wasn't going to get pregnant. There I was, in living color, a perfect candidate. At 2:30 in the afternoon of the same day, I received a call from the personnel director telling me I was hired. I was now an assistant fashion director.

A Change of Perception

As human beings, we all have certain basic needs, no matter what our age. We have a need to be loved and to love. We have a need to be accepted, respected, approved of and appreciated. We also need to be involved and to look forward to something. That's what makes us feel good about ourselves.

Unfortunately, we often treat ourselves more critically, more destructively than we do others. We don't give ourselves credit for the things we do. On the contrary, many of us do ourselves an injustice by discrediting, minimizing and belittling our abilities and our accomplishments.

Even after years of living and acquiring new strengths, we don't update our attitude toward ourselves. We go on berating ourselves, keeping up an endless commentary about life, our feelings and our inadequacies.

We make a habit of comparing ourselves with others. When we do this, we usually come out second best. The fallacy is that we compare our weaknesses with other people's strengths. Yet, we can't excel in everything. There will always be someone who can do something better than we can, who is more educated, more knowledgeable, more talented in certain areas, someone who is smarter, younger. The list is endless. No wonder we feel as we do. When we continue to focus on what we believe to be our weaknesses, rather than our strengths, we will eventually expect less and settle for less, because we believe we're less than others.

Our position in life is not the result of inferior abilities, but of the inferior opinion we have of ourselves. We exaggerate the extent of our inferiority, consequently, we let it cloud our vision and hold us back from the accomplishments that are well within our reach.

There comes that moment when we have to take a long, hard look at our lives. If we find we are at an impasse, and we want to start moving again, we must first admit to ourselves that we're dissatisfied.

I experienced that moment of truth and came face to face

with the biggest obstacle that kept me from moving forward. I was the obstacle, or more accurately, the perception I had of myself.

I learned some valuable lessons from all of those experiences. Probably the most important one was that where I was in life was not the result of my inferior abilities, but of the inferior opinion I had of myself. I had talents and skills that were certainly marketable, but I had not valued them. I had believed myself to be inept, incompetent and useless in the world of business among the important men and women who were smart, worked in offices, carried briefcases, and had power. I was just a homemaker.

It's all too common to feel that others are achieving more and are more confident than we are. That's only because we're aware of our own failures and insecurities while they hide theirs. A low self-image warps how we perceive ourselves and steals our confidence.

Many of us are living frustrated lives because we take a doubtful attitude toward ourselves and, as a result, toward life in general. If we don't have the things we want in life, if we aren't who we would like to be, we need to look to our thoughts and the words we use when talking to others.

We all have abilities we don't know about. We can do things we never dreamed we could do. It's usually only when forced by necessity, that we rise to the occasion and do the things that in the past seemed impossible. Our problem is that we tend to minimize the things we can accomplish, the goals we can reach

The attitude we have about ourselves is vitally important, not only for the quality of our performance in the business world, but also for the outcome of our entire lives. The limitations we feel, the goals we set for ourselves, and our whole approach to life is strongly influenced by the image we have of ourselves. Our self image, at this very moment, is either our greatest asset or our greatest liability.

Many of our problems are problems of a low self-image and the lack of self-confidence. With the loss of these qualities, we don't feel as good about ourselves, and we are not as sure about ourselves as we once were. That is why having a high self-image is so important. It is something we all need. We need it because:

- It is at the very center of our being.
- It increases our chance of finding happiness.
- It affects how we see the world, and our place in it.
- Our self-image affects the choices we make, choices about what we will do with our lives.
- The level of our self-image affects basically everything we think, say and do.

Your Belief Is Your Reality

A Native American fable tells about a young brave who took an egg from an eagle's nest and put it in a chicken yard. The egg hatched and the eagle grew up among the chickens, pecking in the ground for food just as they did, scratching in the dust as he watched the others do. One day he looked up and saw an eagle flying high above him. He felt his wings tremble and said to one of the chickens, "I wish I could do that." "Don't be a fool," the chicken said, "Only an eagle can fly so high." Feeling ashamed of his longing, the eagle went back to scratching in the dust, never again to question what he believed to be his assigned place on earth.

We cannot achieve success in this life if we constantly believe we are unworthy. We must remove the thoughts that do not contribute to a good opinion of who we are--thoughts that diminish us as individuals. It was Emerson who said, "Make the most of yourself, for that is all there is of you."

To change things in our lives is a matter of changing our beliefs about them. It is the key to unlocking the hidden potential dormant within us. We need to keep reminding ourselves, "It isn't who I am, it's who I think I am that sets the boundaries of my accomplishments."

You will have a relationship with yourself, all your life. So it's time to promise to:

- Love yourself the way you are now.
- Always acknowledge that you are enough just the way you are.
- Be your own best friend.
- Love, honor and cherish yourself
- Be comfortable being yourself, not what you perceive others would like you to be.

Your self-image is built on how you feel about yourself, and to some extent how you think others feel about you.

When we put limitations on ourselves, we don't allow ourselves into the boundless realm of creative thought where we can envision wonderful experiences, a new career or a satisfying lifestyle. Our thought patterns bind us to a life of limitation and mediocrity. We need to stop exaggerating the abilities of others, while criticizing our own lack, and begin to focus on our abilities, talents and strengths.

Start building a new concept, a new mental picture of yourself by applying some "don'ts:"

- Don't give in to negatives. Replace self-criticism with positive self-talk. If you fill your mind with confident thoughts, you leave no room for self-doubt.
- Don't compare yourself with others. Come from your strengths, not your weaknesses, when dealing with others.
- Don't compete with others. To be better than some one else is not your goal. Keep up with yourself. You're not in competition with anyone else.
- Don't try to be a carbon copy of those around you. Establish a sense of your own identity.
- Don't spend time worrying about you. Listen more closely to others. You'll find they have some of the same doubts and fears as you do. You need to be aware that what you see in others is only the sur face of self-assurance. You would judge yourself less harshly if you realized that everyone has similar feelings of inadequacies that you do.

You are never too old to change. Creating a new self-image will release your talents and abilities. Within you is the power to do what you want to do. This power becomes available to you as soon as you change the beliefs you have about yourself. With confidence you will feel free to be yourself and to express yourself.

It's Your Move

Write your thoughts on each of these questions.

* What are some of the negative things you say to yourself and others?

_____

_____

_____

* Are you in the habit of comparing yourself to others? Explain how.

_____

_____

_____

* How are you affected by other people's opinion? Explain how.

_____

_____

_____

Remember, as soon as you alter your perception of yourself and your future, you and your future begin to change.

Just to Remind You...

As human being we all need to be loved, to be accepted, respected, approved of and appreciated.

- Be involved and have something to look forward to
  makes us feel good about ourselves.

- Update your attitude toward yourself and stop
  comparing yourself to others.

- Who is your biggest critic? Focus on your
  strengths, not your weaknesses. Stop believing
  you're less than others.

- The limitations you feel, the goals you set for
  yourself and your whole approach to life is strongly
  influenced by the image you have of yourself.

- We all have a picture inside of us of whom we
  think we are. Everything we do is always
  consistent with that image.

- Read self-help books, attend lectures and workshops to give you different ideas and to help you
  change how you feel about yourself.

- Visualize good things happening to you!

- We all have abilities we don't know about.

- Attitude is everything. Low self-esteem warps how we perceive ourselves.

- When you put limitations on yourself, you don't allow yourself into the boundless realm of creative thought where you can envision wonderful experiences, a new career, or a satisfying lifestyle.

- You're never too old to change. Creating a new self-image will release your talents and abilities.

- Within you is the power to do what you want to do. This power becomes available to you as soon as you change the beliefs you have about yourself.

- You need to keep reminding yourself, "It isn't who I am, it's who I think I am that sets the boundaries of my accomplishments."

Chapter 4

"The greatest revolution in our generation
is the discovery that human being,
by changing the inner attitude of their minds,
can change the outer aspects of their lives."

– William James

Think About It

If you were asked today, "Do you want more out of life," you would not hesitate to give a resounding "Yes." You would probably say, "I want more love, more opportunities for success, more financial independence." And if you were asked, "What is the biggest obstacle that prevents you from having more," a perceptive answer would be "I am."

If we don't have the conditions we want, there is no one else to blame. We can't avoid the responsibility of what we experience in our daily lives because everything we experience is largely the result of our own thinking.

To change the quality of our lives, we must change the quality of our thinking. We need to become aware of the things we think about. It is our past thoughts and beliefs that brought us to this moment. What we choose to think, believe and say will create the next moment, the next day, the next month and the years ahead. Thought is the most dynamic, most creative element we have to work with. If it isn't controlled, it can be the most destructive force in our lives.

No one can prevent us from being successful, at any time in our lives, except ourselves. Whatever thoughts, attitudes or opinions we impress on our mind will be what we experience.

Talking to Ourselves

It is through our inner dialogue that we make decisions, set goals for ourselves, feel pleased and satisfied, depressed or discontent. In short, our behavior, our feelings, our inner dialogue influences our sense of self-worth.

So what have you been telling yourself today? Have you fretted about your future, chided yourself about your past mistakes and wrong decisions, or have you praised and supported yourself?

If you don't remember what you said to yourself today, you're not alone. We're not aware of the many negative things we say to ourselves. Why? Self-talk is so familiar to us. It's exactly this feedback that limits our successes and keeps us from feeling good about ourselves. Our inner dialogue has the power to immobilize us. We need to notice the negative things we say to ourselves and to others in casual conversations, such as:

"Nothing is working out for me."
"I just don't have the energy."
"I'm not good enough."
"I don't know enough.
"I'm too old to change."

"I'm not the person I used to be."
"I don't have confidence in myself."

To unleash our full potential, we need to rid ourselves of the things we think and say that diminish us as individuals. We need to change the dialogue of the voice within that insists, "You're not smart enough," "You're not attractive enough," "You're not creative enough."

It is essential that we consciously discard these negative phrases and thoughts, as they bring us the very opposite of what we want.

We need to be aware, at all times, that we have incredible power within us. When we speak, think or maintain a destructive or negative thought, such as, "Nothing seems to work out for me," or "I'll never be able to do that," we're actually asking this power within to create such conditions in our lives.

Unlike our conscious mind, our subconscious mind is impersonal. It treats everything we say with the same indifference. It just accepts and obeys and brings back to us the things we think about, talk about, and believe to be true. If we want this powerful, creative mind to work in our favor, we need to stop giving it the wrong commands.

Most of us are unaware of the power we use against ourselves every day. We go on living unsatisfactory lives when, in reality, we have powerful resources to change the things that don't make us happy. Our thinking determines what we will accomplish, or fail to accomplish. Ask yourself: "What are you giving power to?"

- Your weaknesses?
- How bad you feel?
- How awful life is?

Our life, through our thoughts, is in our own hands. We can make it whatever we desire. We're free to build or destroy, to be strong or weak, happy, or miserable. It's all a matter of channeling our thoughts.

It doesn't matter when or where the thought comes, whether it filters into our consciousness in the silence of our bedroom, or comes to us in the noise of a busy day. If we hold on to the thought, it becomes a part of us. And that thought, in time, will become a reality in our lives.

We all live in a limitless world where anything is possible. But do we really believe that? We may say yes, and then listen as a friend talks about the likelihood of all the negative things that could happen. And in a heartbeat, we begin to worry about the future.

We need to keep in mind that we create our own prosperity, no matter what the economy is like. Our challenge is to keep our thoughts about our future positive and not to be affected by what other people are thinking or saying. Our thoughts and words create the picture of what we draw to us. It's important to think about what we want rather than what we don't want. We will not get what we want by fearing or disliking the opposite.

Regret: The Time-and-Energy Waster

For some of us, it isn't so much the thoughts we have about the present, it's the thoughts we have about our yesterdays that can give us problems. For example, getting rid of guilt. We carry the memory of past mistakes and failures, and we waste time and emotional energy, checking out our yesterdays.

The biggest mistake of all is to continue to recall past mistakes and failures. We need to release these memories. They belong to our past, and guilt holds us to the past. Everything we have ever experienced is within our minds. While we can never erase negative experiences, we can keep from giving them life by not giving them the energy of thought. These three steps may set things right for you:

1. **Forgive yourself** for all the past mistakes and wrong decisions. Whatever you did or didn't do, forgive yourself, close the door and get on with your life.
2. **Absolve yourself of guilt.** Harboring guilt will eat away at your self-esteem. You need to let go of the "I should have," "Why didn't I?" or "If only." They serve no purpose in your life today.
3. Finally, promise yourself now, this moment, **to travel light.** Leave behind your excess baggage such as mistakes, failures, anger, resentments and regrets.

Forgive yourself when you look back. It doesn't matter how many times you failed, successful tries are important and should be remembered. Use your mistakes, failures, wrong choices and faulty decisions as a way of learning, and then release them, they have served their purpose.

You may not be able to resolve all your old conflicts, but you can diminish their effects. Once you become aware of the price you pay to hold onto them, you can refuse to give them new life.

When you find yourself burdened by unpleasant thoughts of the past, *STOP*! Say to yourself, "I did the best I could do at the time, and I release these thoughts now." In time, as you continue to use this affirmation, it will become easier to replace negative thoughts with the good things you really like in your life today.

Cause and Effect

When we accept life as it unfolds one day at a time, without consciously taking control of our thoughts, we're turning our life over to our mind's conditioning. We need to change the thoughts that we've accepted over the years: "This is the way it is." "Nothing is going to change for me." "This is the way it'll always be." "There is no way out." **Thinking the right thoughts** is the basis of all accomplishments, success, self-confidence and happiness.

Down through the centuries, teachers and philosophers have told us about the effects of thought upon our circumstances and ourselves. In The Book of Proverbs, it states, "As a Man thinketh in his heart, so is he." (As a woman thinketh in her heart, so is she.) Buddha said, "What you think, you become." In the writings of the Upanishads, it says, "As one's thinking is, such one becomes."

In later years, and along those same lines, James Allen, who wrote, *"As a Man Thinketh,"* said, "You are what you think. You attract what you think. Your life is a product of your thoughts and beliefs, and nothing in the world will change this fact. To alter your life, the only course open to you, is to alter your thinking."

These are simple words. They were not meant to confuse us. Through these words we become aware that thought is a vital living force that we can use to mold and to shape our lives. They assure us of a life of hope, realizing that whatever we want to be or achieve is possible.

Our thoughts determine who we are, what we are, and what we will become. We alone decide what we think; therefore we decide the course of our lives.

No matter how much we may wish to shift responsibility for our actions to others at times, we live in a world of cause and effect. The elements of success or failure are within all of us. We create our own inner world and consequently our outer world.

The Impact of Our Attitudes

It isn't the profound thought we may have during the course of day that affects us; it's the little repetitious thoughts we have each and every day.

A new study suggests that having more positive thoughts about growing older may help us live a longer life. One of the findings of the study reported in the Journal of Personality and Social Psychology led by psychologist Becca Levy of Yale University, was that people who had positive attitudes about aging lived more that 7.6 years longer than those with negative perceptions. The study was done over a period of 23 years and involved 660 adults, 50 years and older.

We always have the option of choosing what we think. No one willingly engages in negative and destructive thoughts or feelings. It is usually a pattern we have set unconsciously. However, each negative thought impressed in our mind, brings us the very opposite of what we really want.

Here is another example of how our thoughts have an impact on us. A woman is reading a classified ad in the newspaper that tells of an opportunity for a mature woman who is bright, ambitious and has the ability to communicate well with others. Jane is 57 years old and not satisfied with her present job. She thinks about the ad for a few minutes, and then decides that they are probably looking for someone with more experience and more ability than she has, and there's no point in answering it.

When you tell yourself you cannot do something, you then either don't make an attempt (or you make a half-hearted attempt), and tell yourself you knew all along you couldn't do it.

If you were to review the thoughts you entertained or the emotions you felt today, would you want each one imprinted on your mind? Could you use every thought to further your purpose, or would half of your day's thoughts and emotions balance the other half, positive and negative, so that tonight you're no further ahead than you were yesterday?

If we view our later years as a time of poor health, boredom and social isolation, we consciously or unconsciously aim ourselves in that direction. On the other hand, if we expect to live a long life filled with good health, fulfilling activities and social usefulness, we may direct ourselves toward those more hopeful possibilities. It's called "a self-fulfilling prophecy."

In considering our future, we must be concerned only with the belief we have in it. If we believe we are too old, that we have no talents or nobody wants us, then these become the convictions accepted by our subconscious mind.

Those thoughts, uppermost in our minds, will determine our character, our work, and our everyday life. The way we walk, talk and dress, all reflect our way of thinking. What we exhibit outwardly, we are inwardly.

Affirmations: A Method for Change

In the past, I had always told myself and others, "I'm afraid to stand up and speak." I said it because it was a fact. The fear of public speaking had been with me for as long as I can remember. Each time I had to give a report or stand up and say anything other than my name in front of a group of people, my hands shook, my heart would begin to beat wildly, and my knees refused to lock.

When I started working as a fashion coordinator, I had no problem putting fashion shows together. It was second nature to me. But I could not stand up and give the commentary. The fashion director always took over and gave the commentary for me.

Through a seminar called Executive Dynamics, I learned about affirmations and realized I was reinforcing the fear of public speaking through years of negative suggestions. I stopped making the statement "I'm afraid to stand up and speak," and started affirming, "I am an excellent speaker, well-prepared, logical and completely at ease before any group." I repeated this affirmation five times every morning and every night. As I said the affirmation, I pictured myself before an audience feeling at ease and confident. Slowly, I noticed a change. It became easier for me to stand up before a group of people and speak.

When I was 50 years old, I became a motivational speaker. Making daily affirmations helped me lose my fear and nervousness. I no longer have to cope with the paralyzing fear of public speaking. In fact, today I enjoy it immensely.

The subconscious mind is so powerful and so subject to suggestion that in affirmations we have a tool of extraordinary power. An affirmation is a declaration of who we are or can be. Through affirmations, we can raise our self-image, conquer our fears and become confident. The subconscious mind is extremely receptive and can be convinced of any premise we present it, true or false, negative or positive.

Emil Coue, a French pharmacist living during the early part of the twentieth century, was considered a great authority on the power of suggestion. He astonished the world with the medical results he obtained through the power of suggestion, rather than through the ingestion of pills and syrups as requested by his clientele. He suggested a simple affirmation, "Every day in every way I am getting better and better." He helped thousands in France, as well as throughout the world.

If we don't have the things we want, if we aren't the person we would like to be, we need to take an inventory of our thoughts and the words we use when talking to ourselves and others. Our thoughts create our life.

It stands to reason that if your present situation is the result of past negative suggestions, you can reverse the pattern. If you affirm, "I am shy," "I am disorganized," "I am unsuccessful," you are making these undesired conditions a reality. On the other hand, if you say, "I am confident," "I am well organized," "I am successful," you'll eventually live up to those claims.

We receive only what we give. Our thoughts, deeds and words return to us eventually, and with astounding accuracy. William James said, "We alone, of all the creatures of the earth, can change our own pattern. We alone are the architects of our destiny."

Affirmations are like seeds planted in your subconscious mind. Given time, they will become a reality in your life. To affirm is to state it is so, and as you maintain this attitude of mind as true, regardless of all evidence to the contrary, you will gradually change.

One of the surest ways to become confident is through affirmation. If you consciously follow the method of daily affirmation even for a short time, it will produce satisfying results in your life. The affirmation to achieve self-confidence is, "I am completely relaxed and self-assured in all situations and with all people." With confidence you will become more relaxed, more assertive and enjoy life more.

Affirmations can be said while sitting in a relaxed, comfortable position in a chair, or they can be said while lying in bed, both before going to sleep and after waking up in the morning. It's important to say each affirmation five times and in the present tense.

Affirmations are a simple and effective way to bring about wonderful changes. To be successful, it is essential to believe that results will follow.

Suggested Basic Affirmations:

> "I like myself unconditionally."
> "I am 100 percent alive by thinking, speaking and acting with great enthusiasm."

Suggested Affirmations for Personal Growth:

> "I have an excellent memory."
> "I am well organized in all areas of my life."
> "I face all my problems with courage and solve them easily."
> "I am an excellent speaker, well-prepared, logical and completely at ease before any group."

Suggested Affirmations for Better Health:

> "I possess abundant energy and draw upon it at will."
> "I am easily able to relax."
> "Every day in every way I am getting better and better."

The moving force of "I am...I have...I can" will bring dynamic dimensions to your life. What you will become in the weeks, months and years ahead will depend on the thoughts, beliefs and attitudes you hold from this day forward.

It's Your Move

Ask yourself: Do I consistently make the following statements? (Check the ones you often say.)

_____ "I'm disorganized."

_____ "I'm always late."

_____ "I'm afraid to make a change."

_____ "I'm not smart enough to do that."

_____ "I don't have the energy."

_____ "I don't have the talent."

_____ "I don't have the confidence."

_____ "I don't know enough."

_____ "I don't have any ambition."

_____ "I feel like the best years are behind me."

_____ "I feel bored."

_____ "I feel inferior when I'm with others."

You can literally talk yourself into a negative state of mind, if you keep using "down" words, instead of "up" words. In the Bible, Isaiah, Chapter 55, Verse 11, it says: "So shall my words be that goeth forth out of my mouth. They shall not return unto me void, but they shall accomplish that which I purpose and prosper in that for which I sent it."

Remember, within us lies the cause of whatever enters our lives, and the effect is what we live with. This moment now is your point of power wherein you can change yourself and your life.

Just to Remind You...

Everything we experience is largely the result of our own thinking. To change our life, we must change our thinking.

- We aren't aware of our negative phrases and thoughts.

- No one can prevent us from being successful, except ourselves.

- Our inner dialogue has the power to immobilize us. Negative self-talk so familiar to us, will limit our success and keep us from feeling good about ourselves.

- Our thinking determines what we will accomplish, or fail to accomplish.

- What are you giving power to?

- Do you believe you are living in a limitless world where everything is possible?

- Your challenge is to keep your thoughts about your future positive and not be affected by what other people are thinking and saying.

- Time and emotional energy are wasted dwelling on past mistakes. Release them! Forgive yourself.

- Thinking the right thoughts is the basis of all accomplishments, success, self-confidence and happiness.

- Our thoughts determine who we are, what we are, and what we will become.

- Positive thoughts about growing older will help us to live longer.

- Through affirmations, we can raise our self-image, conquer our fears and become confident.

- Affirmations are a tool of extraordinary power, a declaration of who we are or can be. They are like seeds planted in our subconscious and can bring about wonderful changes.

- This moment NOW is your point of power wherein you can change yourself and your life.

Chapter 5

*"One of the wonderful things about
being alive is that it is never too late...
to write a book, to learn a language, to travel,
to buy a house or to make a friend."*

– Phyllis A. Whitney, 1903-born

Encore! Encore!

At every age a person's life deserves fulfillment, purpose and meaning. Since most people don't look forward to aging, the tendency is to avoid planning ahead for the last third of life. The important thing is not where we were, or where we are, but where we want to be. Life holds no real satisfaction until we experience and express those things that fulfill us.

There are two ways to face the future. One is with apprehension; the other is with anticipation. We face the future with anticipation when we have set definite objectives that excite us. Many people go through life getting so little out of it. They don't know what they want. David Campbell, Ph.D. said, "If you don't know where you're going, you'll probably end up somewhere else." In the past, the older you got, the less you were expected to try new things, meet new people, or experiment with new ways of living. You were definitely not suppose to go back to school, fall in love, begin a new career.

For life to have purpose, it must be planned and directed. Unless short-term and long-term goals are defined, we will achieve only a small fraction of what is possible. If we don't think about and choose what we want to do, we risk getting bogged down in a lifestyle or circumstances that keep us forever sidetracked from our dreams.

The quickest way to grow old is to stop having goals, to say: "I have nothing to do," "I'm too old," "It's too late," "My life is over." In reality, we create our own feelings of emptiness when we just drift. There's no purpose or vitality to our life without goals. When we look to the future and see possibilities, we maintain a sound sense of ourselves and of our place in the world around us.

The last third of life offers a great deal of opportunity. If you knew you were going to live another twenty, thirty or forty more years, what would you do? Where would you begin? Would you go back to college, take evening classes, participate in workshops on self-development, or do research.

Yet many of us wake each morning with a feeling of emptiness and face a day that lacks meaning or direction. We reason this void is because the children are gone, the job is just a job, or that in retirement, life holds no meaning.

In reality, we create our own feelings of emptiness when we just drift with life; the easiest thing in the world is to drift without purpose or direction. Without an objective, life becomes dull, boring and monotonous.

It's Never Too Late

There are at least three good reasons to work during our retirement years: because we want to, we have to, or we want to and have to.

A recent AARP study found that 63 percent of pre-retirees expected to work at least part time during retirement, and another 5 percent said they were never going to retire, period.

The pre-retirees listed all the usual reasons for continuing to work:

- Stay mentally active (87 percent).

- Do something fun or enjoyable (71 percent).

- Be around people (58 percent).

When asked for just one reason, however, both the pre-retirees and the retirees surveyed, cited the need for money more than any other factor.

Career expert Martin Yate, author of *Resumes That Knock 'em Dead, said*, "If you already retired and want to get back to work:

1. Consider returning to school. In particular, if you aren't comfortable using computers, take a course at the local community college to catch up.

2. Limit your resume to two pages or less and tailor it to the kind of work you want to do. Rather than list every job you've ever held, sum them up in one paragraph. Focus instead on the skills you've honed over your career.

3. Ask questions and focus on how your skills would be a good fit. They don't care that you were a senior VP at IBM. They want to know how you can help them. Everyone who ever gets hired for any job is hired to solve a problem."

Many examples exist about creative, dynamic and productive older people who made a success of their business careers after 60. Frank Lloyd Wright, for example, designed most of his buildings between the ages of sixty-two and ninety-one. At 64, Colonel Harlan Sanders, the founder of Kentucky Fried Chicken, decided to franchise the name and the method of making chicken after a new highway was built that bypassed his own restaurant. He traveled around the country selling the concept. By the time he was 74, he had sold 638 franchises. Grandma Moses started painting when she was 79. She illustrated *T'was the Night Before Christmas* when she was 100. When asked why she started painting so late in life, she said, "At 79 I was too old to work in the fields, but I was too young to sit on the porch." That reminds me of a remark made by Arthur Scheslinger Jr., regarding his age. He said, "Every time I contemplate on being 73, I'm shocked. I never feel 73. Most of the time I feel like I'm forty, occasionally I feel like I'm 90, but I never feel 73."

It has been said that people can be divided into three groups. Those who make things happen, those who watch things happen, and those who wonder what happened.

Elaine Stindt was 41 years old when she decided she would like to learn to play the harp. She had been interested in music from an early age. When she learned to play the piano, she remembers lifting the music rack on the old upright piano to pluck the strings. "Perhaps it was a sign of things to come," she said.

Elaine gives credit to her harp teacher, Kathy Kienzle, who always encouraged her to be the best she could be.

"Not only did Elaine bring a remarkable degree of determination to her lessons, she was unusual in other ways," recalls Ms. Kienzle, chair of MacPhail's string and harp department. "Every week, she would arrive at MacPhail loaded with new material culled from the music files at Schmitt Music Center in Minneapolis. She haunted music seminars and workshops, looking for new work. She even equipped her computer with a program to arrange piano and choral music for flute and harp. Of course, she practiced with a fervor approaching the religious."

Despite that zeal, Elaine said that her earliest recitals were characterized by perspiration and great trembling. When people would ask how long she had played, she thought they were insinuating that someone her age should be more proficient. She volunteered to play at nursing homes for experience.

When Elaine started playing the harp, she never imagined that it would lead to so many wonderful experiences. "Playing with an orchestra is not easy," she said, "there is more to it than meets the eye. But once you have been 'put through the fire,' it is such a sense of accomplishment. When I listen to orchestral music recordings now, I hear far more of the total sound, elements I never noticed before playing in an orchestra setting." Music has become Elaine's life's journey. "I've heard so many people say, "I wish I could do that," she said. "Sure you can sit and wish, but it takes extra effort to sit and learn new things, when you're over 40. " I always say, "Go for it, what do you have to lose?"

Once we've decided that being involved is what keeps us alive and happy, it's up to us to find out how to make the adjustments. Ask yourself: "What is possible in my life now? Possibility creates excitement. It's never too late to learn or do something new. It doesn't matter what form it takes.

Creative Solutions

In the theater there is a well-known precept: "Almost anyone can write a first act, but it takes a playwright to write a second act…and a genius to create a third act." We don't have to be geniuses to write our own third act.

When we're trying to find the answer to the question: "What am I going to do?" "What can I do?" we must look to something other than the conscious mind for the answer.

A great deal has been written about how insight seems to come from an unseen creative force. Each of us has had the experience of struggling with a problem or question to which we could not seem to find a satisfying answer. When we finally gave up, or we turned our attention to some other routine activity, then suddenly the solution has flashed into our mind.

Thomas Paine, referring to the source of his great storehouse of knowledge, said, "Any person who has made an observation on the state of progress of the human mind by observing his own, cannot but have observed that there are two distinct classes of what are called thoughts: those that we produce in ourselves by reflection and the act of thinking, and those that bolt into the mind of their own accord."

A simple example is what happens when we forget a name. We first try consciously to recall it, often unsuccessfully, when we finally give up trying, the name surfaces. Since many of us have experienced this flash of insight after giving up on a problem, the question it raises is, "How can a person learn to turn on this intuition whenever it is needed?"

The important first step is to focus our conscious minds on the question or problem to solve. We need to study the problem. Dig for facts. Then dismiss it from our mind. Our creative mind works best when there is not too much interference from our conscious mind. In sleep your creative mind has an opportunity to work independently of conscious interference, if you've started working on the problem.

Problem-Solving Techniques

The creative area of the mind will provide the insight to help solve problems, make decisions and help achieve goals. All you need to do is define the problem, decision or goal:

1. Write the problem on a sheet of paper or in a notebook.
2. Gather information regarding the problem.
   a. Your own information.
   b. Written information (magazines or books).
   c. Information you get from others.
3. Work out the problem on paper (pros and cons).
4. If the solution does not present itself, turn it over to the subconscious mind (and forget about it).
5. Get busy with some other activity.

When we give our subconscious mind a problem to solve (one that we have consciously worked on for some time), our mind will accept it, work on it, and give us solutions. We need only to have a firm conviction that results will follow.

We often hear that men get their best ideas while shaving. Some people have their best ideas while doing mundane chores around the house or working in the garden.

The subconscious area of the mind is a reservoir of creative insight and intuition. This is why we should turn over a greater portion of our problems to this creative mind. When we rely more and more on this creative mind to solve our problems and create ideas, we fret less and feel more confident.

To start things moving, ask yourself the following questions:

Am I ready for a change?
What could I lose if I make a change?
What will I gain?
What are my options?

If you are the type whose only thought is to help others, then consider volunteering. Many of the happiest people are engaged in caring enterprises. Studies show that adults who get involved in their communities live longer than their peers who don't volunteer. New friendships and experiences make their lives richer.

If you want to volunteer, think about what interests you most – a cause you're passionate about or an organization that could use your skills, such as your church, or school, library or local museum.

The opportunities for helping others are boundless, and the rewards are greatest when the focus is the needs of others. Albert Schweitzer called such effort "the career of the spirit."

Aging and All That Jazz

Her name is Penelope Ann Morgan Barnett Swartz. She gave me all her names – maiden and both married ones – to let me know that her 51 years have not been altogether boring, but rather, filled with living and all that it can entail.

She is a minister by profession, a calling that didn't come until she was thirty-nine. She started seminary two weeks before her 40th birthday. Penny works as the associate minister for pastoral care in a congregation of about 1500 members. It's a mainline, liberal Protestant church, which is a nice way of saying it has an aging congregation. The majority of her responsibilities involve visiting members who are hospitalized, homebound, or in some type of assisted-living situation. In short, she works with people who are at the crest of the hill, or beyond it, in terms of aging. She said, "Oddly enough, they neither make me feel like a lucky whippersnapper, nor do they instill in me any fear of aging. They're just people like me."

Penny is most conscious of her own aging in two ways. First, the physical changes. She said, "I'm constantly forgetting that I can't read without my glasses anymore, and I'm seriously considering letting my hair go completely gray, when my hairdresser tells me I'm about 80 percent already there. She said that middle-age spread is a reality she could do better about controlling, but she gets out early in the morning and walks over three miles six times a week. The second way she is conscious of her own aging is that her mother's siblings are dying off. Her mother is one of eight children. Her mother will be eighty-four and still works full time, and maintains her own home and garden. She still drives, too, and plans to drive by herself from California to visit Penny in Michigan (with stops along the way)..

Penny is over two years into her second marriage to a great guy and their 'collective' children all are within weeks of being 'out of the house.' "Being an empty nester never sounded so good," she said. "Hubby and I are looking forward to renewing our courtship and playing – in all the fullness of the word."

In the meantime, in addition to church ministry, Penny has discovered the field of spiritual direction and is starting the second of a two-year internship to become a trained spiritual director. "Where that leads me," she said, "I have no idea. God might know, but God's not saying – yet."

She also has an increased desire to write her *Pastor*

Penny novels. "I've have the characters of Valentine Goforth and Liberty McAllister rattling around in my head, and they want out." Although she expects to begin giving them their voices within the next calendar year, she asks herself the question, "Is that productive?" Her answer, "I don't know, but it's interesting."

She reminisces about being a kid riding a bus to school. It would pick up kids from all grades – kindergarten through high school. "When I was in fourth grade," she said, "I remember sitting on that bus looking at the high school girls in their trim, short-skirted dresses, with their nylons and pumps, their hair ratted and coifed. They wore makeup! And I knew what I was going to look like when I grew up and was in high school. They were my idols. But by the time I was in high school, I didn't look anything like them. The times had changed. More importantly, I was becoming my own person – not a carbon copy of a memory.

"I really know only a few things with any certainty," Penny said, "and one of them is this: Life can be over without a moment's notice, so live it fully and to the very best of your ability – whatever that level is. Fear is not of God, and I won't go quietly into the night. Live! That's what we're here for."

It's important for all of us to accept the fact that maturity does not mean being washed up at 60... or for that matter, 80. Feeling dissatisfied is reason enough for wanting to change the way life is going for us.

If our life seems unrewarding, it is an indication that we have unfulfilled needs. Numerous examples exist of achievements in every profession, the arts, literature and technology, by people who are over 60. There isn't any reason why we cannot remain creative as long as we live.

To get started, think about what you want out of life. Ask yourself: "What is it that I want to have accomplished by the end of my life?" List all the things you want to do, to have, to be, whether in a career, or in your personal life. Don't stop to consider whether it will be difficult or easy to accomplish these desires. Just write from a gut feeling, no matter how unrealistic the goal may seem right now. These coming years can offer more potential, more achievement and more enjoyment, than any in the past.

Motivational speaker Les Brown reminds us that, "You are never too old to set another goal or to dream a new dream."

It Ain't Over Till It's Over

This is also a wonderful time to make some powerful inner changes. Such as:

- Become unattached to stuff.

- Forgive everyone, including yourself.

- Give up criticism.

- Give away your guilt.

- Promise yourself you are no longer taking on anyone's baggage.

As long as we live, we need to have hope, dreams and aspirations. With health and energy, anyone can have a passion to do something more in this lifetime. In the final analysis, everyone is too old for something, but no one is too old for everything.

It's Your Move

Write your thoughts on each of these questions.

- Am I ready for a change? Explain why.

_____

_____

_____

- Where do I want to be in five years?

_____

_____

_____

- What would I lose if I make a change?

_____

_____

_____

- What will I gain?

  _____

  _____

  _____

- Do I have the confidence to make the changes
  necessary for achieving my goals?

  _____

  _____

  _____

- What are my options?

  _____

  _____

  _____

At the beginning of the 20th century, the number of people who lived beyond the age of 60 was relatively small, and there was little concern over what to do with those added years.

Today, however, it's a different story. Ahead of us lies twenty or thirty more productive years after age 60. The simple fact is that it's never too late to make life meaningful. We have the time to start over, to change, and to begin again.

It is up to you to take a realistic look at yourself and the opportunities that may lie ahead of you, and take action to ensure that your future will be a fulfilling one. David Ogilivy, an advertising executive said, "The secret of a long life is double careers. One to about sixty, then another for the next thirty years."

Just to Remind You...

Remember, to live a long, fulfilling life you need to have direction, drive and a sense of purpose. At every age a person's life deserves fulfillment, purpose and meaning.

- Since most people do not look forward to aging, the tendency is to avoid planning ahead for the last third of life. The important thing is not *where we were*, or *where we are*, but *where we want to be*.

- Life holds no real satisfaction until we experience and express those things that fulfill us.

- There are two ways to face the future. One is with apprehension; the other is with anticipation.

- For life to have purpose, it must be planned and directed.

- The quickest way to grow old is to stop having goals.

- If you knew you were going to live another twenty, thirty or forty more years, what would you do? Where would you begin?

- It has been said that people can be divided into three groups. Those who make things happen, those who watch things happen, and those who wonder what happened.

- Our life will have no purpose or vitality without goals.

- We create our own feelings of emptiness when we just drift with life.

- When we give our subconscious mind a problem to solve (one that we have consciously worked on for some time), our mind will accept it, work on it, and give us solutions. We need only to have a firm conviction that results will follow.

- The subconscious area of the mind is a reservoir of creative insight and intuition. When we rely on this creative mind to solve problems and create ideas, we fret less and feel more confident.

- Everyone is too old for something, but no one is too old for everything.

- In living longer we have second and third chances and opportunities to begin again.

Chapter 6

*"If you live your life by setting and achieving
goals one right after the other,
you will achieve more in five years
than most people do in a lifetime."*

– William James, American psychologist
and philosopher

I Still Want More!

During the course of our lives, many of us are caught
between the desire to have more, and settling for less.
Although goals are vital to the psychological well-being of
every individual, many of us continue to live without them.
We just live life as it comes along, one day at a time. When
we do this, we are on free fall...we let whatever happens,
happen.

Many people, after 60, may feel that they have neither
the time nor the energy to make changes or plan for the
future. They hesitate to take up anything new. But if we realize that without goals, life has no direction or purpose, we
will begin to understand that establishing clearly defined
goals is the most important step to take.

It's time to ask yourself, "Am I working on long-term
goals, short-term goals, or am I just trying to get through the
day?" One of our greatest responsibilities is to determine

what we really want in this life. That responsibility is ours alone.

When we believe something is impossible, our mind goes to work to prove us correct. But, when we believe, really believe something can be done, our minds work for us and help find a way. Eliminate the word "impossible" from your thoughts, beliefs and vocabulary. Impossible is a failure word. The thought, "It's impossible," sets off a chain reaction of other thoughts to prove you are right.

Find Your Passion

Think of something you have wanted to do, but felt you couldn't. Make a list of the reasons why you want to and why you can do it. Many people defeat their desires simply because they concentrate on why they can't do it, rather than why they can.

Believing that something can be accomplished paves the way for creative solutions and is basic to creative thinking. These suggestions can help you bridge the gap from "I can't" to "I will."

- Use encouraging words, such as "Possible!" "Great!" and "It *will* work!"

- Become receptive to new ideas. Replace thoughts such as, "I can't do it," and "It's useless," to "I can do it," "I can try," and "Why not me?"

- Expand your thinking. Think big thoughts. The belief in big results is the driving force. The "okay, I'll give it a try, but I don't think it'll work" attitude will produce failure.

- Associate with people who encourage you to think of new ideas and look at new ways of doing things.

Success in life depends on identifying what would fulfill us, and then acting on it. "This time, like all times, is a very good one," Emerson said, "if we but know what to do with it." A reader wrote to columnist Abigail Van Buren telling of her desire to go back to college to study medicine. She reasoned that it would take seven years to finish, and by that time she would be forty-three years old. Dear Abby replied, "And how old will you be in seven years, if you don't go back to college."

It has been said that if we want something, we need to make a space for it. If we let go of old ideas, old habits and old ways of thinking, we have space for new things and new events to light up our lives.

Get What You Want

Beverly Harris decided to go into business five years ago. "My children started school, and I was home alone," she said. "I hate housework. I thought, I'd rather go out and work and have someone else clean my house."

Her only qualification was teaching elementary school. "I had just sent my children off to school, and I really didn't want to spend the day with twenty-six other children," Beverly said. "The only other thing I could do was cook. I enjoy cooking for a large group, making all the fancy dishes and beautiful desserts. As a result, instead of doing the housework, I hosted large, costly parties, simply to keep occupied."

People started asking if she would help them. Beverly thought that was wonderful, because now it would be their expense – not hers. After awhile, she was doing so much work on their parties, it became ridiculous. Beverly decided if she was going to do it, it might as well pay. That's when she became a professional caterer.

"I was in business a very short time when I realized that the only way to make it profitable was to become a kosher caterer, as there was a need. I went to Boston to get a license. Being a kosher caterer is probably one of the most difficult things to accomplish. They are ultra strict," Beverly said. "You are governed by the dietary laws, which for many years were health laws. Things have progressed over the years, but you still must abide by them because the rabbis say you must. They are part of the religion and people live by them. If you are going to cater to these people, you must also abide by these dietary laws."

Beverly went before a board of twenty-five rabbis and the first thing they said was: This shouldn't be a business for a nice girl like you. You don't want to be involved in this. You don't need this aggravation. "I sat there, and I decided as I looked at them, I'm going to do it and sooner or later you are going to give me a license. They could have discouraged me twenty years ago," she said. "I would have been willing to forget the whole thing, figuring, oh well, I'll find something else to do."

Here was this board of rabbis speaking Hebrew to each other, which she didn't understand. She was sitting there trying to get her point across and all she heard from them was: "This is a very hard business. This is a man's work. This is a man's thing. Go home, take care of your husband and your children." Beverly said, "I sat there and they told me I couldn't do it because I am a woman."

When she returned home, she went to see her rabbi. "I asked him if he would go before the board with me," she said. "He could talk to them because he speaks Hebrew. I told him I didn't understand what they were saying. We went back and, through him, I got my point across. They gave me a conditional license for six months. They wanted to watch me. They were extremely careful to make sure that I followed every rule they had set forth. I really enjoyed doing it, and I didn't find it that difficult. I was brought up in a kosher home so I knew basically what they were talking about."

Beverly worked six months on a dairy license. They would not allow her to handle meat at all because it was more complicated. But she discovered in six months that there wasn't any money in dairy. "The people who came to me," she said, "were looking for the small, inexpensive-type function, instead of weddings, for which they wanted roast beef."

She went back to the board and told them that she wanted to handle meat. To do this involved building another kitchen. "You are not allowed to have dairy and meat kitchens on the same floor for fear that some of the utensils will be mixed together. I really had to assess whether to go on because it would be a very costly venture. When my husband and I talked it over, he said, 'Go ahead.' Today, we have an extremely successful kosher catering business."

A Dream in the Attic

Every day thousands of people bury good ideas because they are afraid to act on them. *Tomorrow*, *next week*, *later*, *sometime*, *someday* often are synonymous with *never*. *Now* is the magic word for success.

When people look back over their lives, they regret actions and risks not taken far more than the mistakes they made, even the big ones, this according to a study conducted by Cornell University, where Thomas Gilovich, Ph.D., professor of psychology, found that when we make a decision to do things and they go badly, we suffer intense pain, but only for a brief period of time. Then we begin to adapt to the situation. However, when we don't take the risk, we suffer the pain of inaction and the period of regret is much longer.

The story is told of a middle-aged man who, while rummaging through the attic, found an old notebook from his days as a senior in high school. There in the yellowed pages was the plan he had written for his life and the goals he intended to accomplish. He belatedly realized that all the goals he had listed could indeed have been accomplished. Sadly he just never got started.

One reason few of us will do the great things we had

planned to do, or things we are capable of doing, is because we lock ourselves into schedules each day. Between work and our favorite television programs each night, either we don't make the time, or we're just too tired.

When we plan for a vacation, for instance, we know exactly where we are going and how we will travel. We can estimate how long the trip will take because we know our destination. Most people would never consider getting into their car and driving around aimlessly until vacation time was over.

Yet, so many of us do that with our lives. We divert our energies in many directions, leaving ourselves with little energy, time, or motivation to pursue what we consider most important. A goal is a purpose, an objective. A goal is a clearly defined: This is what I want.

Arlene Williams decided at age 50, to go back into the business world. "Up until that time," she said, "I was just playing at life. My husband was a doctor and I didn't have to work outside of my home. I was happy being home with my children." She was involved in charitable organizations and with her many friends. It was a good life.

Then her husband had needed a heart transplant. She recalled the moment in the hospital's waiting room when they first told her. A social worker looked at her and said, "I want to know if you are up to this situation." Arlene thought to herself, "Are there any other options?"

After her husband recovered, she began a career in real estate. "A lot of mature people have left other careers and gone into the real estate business. It's a great place," she said, "for mature men and women. People tend to trust you more than they do someone who is thirty."

Arlene sings at two church services every Sunday. Then she does her open houses for three hours. Before she started working, she set a goal to keep her family connected. Every Sunday evening, she has her children for dinner. Every Monday, she meets with the same group of women from her neighborhood that she describes as interesting and dynamic. She calls it the "Attitude Adjustment Lunch."

People are always asking Arlene when she will retire. "You need to slow down, take it easy." Arlene's response is, "at some point, I'll say, that's enough, but not yet."

Arlene also makes all her social plans for the year for herself and her husband. She puts the events on her calendar. "One of the most important benefits derived from setting goals and planning how to achieve them," she says, "is that great feeling of expectancy when you know 'something' is happening in your life, and you are making it happen."

A goal stimulates excitement, directs energy, motivates our efforts and delivers results. One of the basic drives leading to achievement is a deep, heart-felt purpose that gives us the strength to encounter adversity without allowing it to deplete our determination to reach a goal. In other words, we don't quit. Added benefits of goal setting are that it:

- Gives purpose to the way we spend our day.
- Creates a sense of anticipation.
- Gives our life direction.

Once we've decided on a goal, there are definite steps to follow to achieve it:

Five Step Plan

1. Desire. Desire is one of our most powerful emotions. It is the driving force within all of us. Desire is the foundation of goal setting and without it, very little is accomplished. To desire deeply is to have singleness of purpose. Desire and need will get us from where we are now to where we want to be. Without it, nothing major can be achieved.

However, strange as it may seem, comparatively few people have a great, burning desire. Most of us are content to go along living in the tiny niches in which we find ourselves. We accept our position in life as something fate has destined. Very seldom do we make a conscious or physical effort to change our situation. Sparked by a burning desire, wonderful things can happen in your life.

A powerful desire will get you from where you are now to where you want to be in the future. So ask yourself this question: "How much do I want what I really want?" A specific goal, backed by a burning desire, becomes a powerful combination. It was Emerson who said, "Beware of what you desire, for you will surely get it."

If you've looked long and hard and find that there is something lacking in your life, ask yourself two other questions:

What am I looking for?

_____

_____

_____

What do I really want in life?

_____

_____

_____

Simple questions, to be sure, but they are probably the most important ones you'll ever ask yourself.

2. Put your goal in writing and be specific. The subconscious mind deals in specifics. If you wrote as your goal, "more money," someone could hand you a few coins, and you would have more money. Whatever you wish to achieve must be written out as a clear statement that provides a solid base from which to unlock the door between daydreams and reality.

Avoid general statements. The mind needs a clear picture of what you desire. In the process of writing out your goal you have made a commitment. Writing your goal on a three by five card will prove beneficial. Read it first thing in the morning and the last thing at night.

3. Give yourself a specific time frame. It's important to decide the length of time it will take to accomplish your goal. If you fail to consider the time factor, you may give up too soon. A target date will give you a sense of urgency.

Don't just mark time. Make a commitment to do at least one thing each day toward achieving your goal. If you add it up, in a month you will have at least thirty things accomplished toward your goal. Multiply that by 12 months, and you'll realize how much you can accomplish in a year.

4. Refrain from discussing your goal with others. A woman who attended one of my seminars told me that she wanted to go into business with her husband. At the time, they had a great opportunity to buy a beauty salon. They were excited about the venture as it was a dream come true.

They made the mistake of talking to some of their good friends about it. Their friend's comments were typical. "You've never had the experience of running a business before." "There are too many beauty salons as it is." "The economy is bad, you risk losing everything."

Only one friend said, "Go for it, what have you got to lose?" In thinking it over, they decided not to go into business. They allowed their friends negative responses to influence them. They realized, too late, that by not going into business at that particular time, they missed their greatest opportunity.

Unless your goal include a special person or family member, talking at length about your plans and goal can diminish your motivation. Sharing your plans with others also creates pressure for you to meet their expectations and makes it more difficult to change your mind. Talking about your plans may invite opinions that can inhibit you from action.

We all look to others for approval because we feel it will give us confidence. When someone says, "You can do it," it strengthens our belief in ourselves. But people, including our friends, don't always give us the approval we had hoped for.

5. Visualize your goal. Visualization is seeing in your mind's eye, conditions or circumstances not as they are, but as you want them to be. It is necessary to have a clearly defined image in your mind of how you desire to be. Imagination is not daydreaming or fantasy. Your imagination plays a great role in achieving your goals. It is creating a real situation, one in the future, and seeing you in that situation.

Imagination is that part of the mind that plays a great role in achieving our objectives. Anything that has ever been accomplished has first been created and imagined in the mind. First is the vision, then the accomplishment.

One of the most common statements of defeat many of us make is, "I can't picture myself doing that." If we are unable to picture success in any of our endeavors, we will rarely obtain it. We all use our imagination unconsciously. When we worry about tomorrow we are imagining, projecting something about an occurrence that has not yet taken place. We say:

- "I'm afraid I won't get the job."
- "I don't think I can pass the test."
- "I'm sure I won't find what I want."

These are all instances of negatively imagining something that hasn't yet taken place. Once we realize that our actions and feeling are the result of our own images and beliefs, we have the lever for change. A mental image provides the basis for everything we do or don't want to happen. Through our imagination and affirmations, we can create a different environment, better our conditions and achieve our goals.

Among the growing body of research on the study of imagery and how it works is the dramatic story of the Swiss Alpine ski team. They were taught the skills of mental rehearsal and practiced them diligently. The skiers were then sent down the grand slalom course, their backpacks filled with equipment to monitor brain waves, heart rate, muscle tension, etc. In the laboratory the next day, the skiers were again hooked up to the monitors and were asked to visualize themselves running the slalom. The physiological responses were exactly the same; visualizing the skiing and actually physically skiing produced the same results.

In his book, *Psycho Cybernetics*, Dr. Maxwell Maltz gives us an explanation for this phenomenon. He says, "Mental pictures offer us an opportunity to practice new traits and attitudes that otherwise we could not do. This is possible because your nervous system cannot tell the difference between an actual experience and one that is vividly imagined."

Be There Now

Success comes from the feeling that we are successful in the present moment. It is not something we may feel someday; when we have reached a goal or have received something we have wanted. We are successful when we identify ourselves with the reality of success, where we are at this moment. Rather than focusing on how far we need to go, before we succeed.

What you have and where you are today is the result of all the choices and decisions you have made to this point in life. Whether they were financial, business, family or relationships, you must get rid of the pictures of times in the past when situations didn't work out as well as you wanted them to.

It doesn't matter how many times you failed. Use your mistakes, failures, wrong choices and faulty decisions as a way of learning. Release them, they have served their purpose.

Everything you have ever experienced is within your mind, and you can never erase it. Whenever you dwell on your mistakes and failures, you give them life; they are then resurrected to become your future. The good news is that the same holds true for your past successes.

Ask yourself: what one achievement has given you the greatest sense of accomplishment. See the incident clearly in your mind. Recall the people who were part of the experience. Remember how they looked, what they said and how you felt during the experience. Become again, in your imagination, the person you were at that time. Then bring your thoughts into the present moment and make plans for your future. Past accomplishments can bring you future success. Not only can you use past successes, you can, through your imagination, picture a different environment, better conditions, or achieve a definite objective.

Now, think of all the reasons why you are closer to getting what you want than you have ever been. And while you are at it, use the power of affirmations and say: "I am a success, and I allow myself to feel successful now."

Here is an exercise in the basic technique of visualization: First think of something you would like. For this exercise choose something simple. Something you can easily imagine attaining. It might be an object you would like to have, an event you would like to happen, or a situation you'd like to find yourself in.

Get in a comfortable position, either sitting or lying down, in a quiet place where you won't be disturbed. Relax your body completely. Starting from your toes and moving up to your scalp, think of relaxing each muscle in your body, letting all tension flow out of your body. Breathe deeply and slowly. Count down slowly from 10 to 1, feeling yourself getting more deeply relaxed with each count.

When you feel completely relaxed, start to imagine the thing you want exactly as you would like it. If it's an object, imagine yourself with the object, holding it, using it, admiring it and enjoying it. If it is a situation or event, imagine yourself there and everything happening just as you want it to. Make the details real to you. You can take a short time or longer time to imagine the scene.

Raise Your Expectations

If you can picture the way you really want your life to be, you vastly improve your chances of achieving your goals. Visualize the things you would like to see in your life. Forget about the negative things that have happened to you. In place of them, mentally create the conditions you would like to see in your life now. Create your own positive image of yourself and make room for new things in your life.

It is necessary to have a clearly defined image in your mind of who you want to be. You need to picture what you really want, not just what you think you can probably have. What you picture in your mind will come to pass when you picture it long enough and clearly.

Visualization is seeing, in your mind's eye, conditions or circumstances not as they are, but as you want them to be. Charles J. Givens, author of *Super Self,* says that, "Your mind never sleeps, at least not your subconscious mind. And it is your subconscious mind that sparks your ability to transform an imagined goal into reality. That's why a great time to visualize goals is while you are on the way to the Land of Nod. Keep a copy of your goals list next to your bed and glance at it before you turn off the light. Then visualize the accomplishment of as many of your goals as possible."

Knowing what you truly want eliminates indecision and confusion. Take the advice of Thomas A. Edison: "If we did all the things we are capable of doing, we would literally astound ourselves." Then consider all aspects of your life: personal, professional, recreational and financial.

Write down what you want. Start moving toward your goal by making the next task you perform a move in the right direction. This list of reminders will help keep you focused and encouraged.

- Write out your plan and each day do at least one task toward accomplishing it.
- Pace yourself to get the best results, and remember, you are not in competition with anyone else.
- Keep your self-talk positive.

- Keep moving forward. Don't be satisfied, with your present accomplishments or progress. When you are satisfied you cease to grow.
- Prepare for whatever you asked for, even when there is no sign of it.
- Always keep your mind on your goal, not on the obstacles.
- Say each day, "I have the talents and abilities necessary to achieve my dreams."
- Visualize your goal each night before you go to sleep and always picture it in the present tense.

Successful living does not come to only those who are the brightest, youngest or the most knowledgeable. A life that is successful is achieved by those who are dedicated, determined and never give up.

It's Your Move

Write your thoughts on each of these questions.

- What do I want to accomplish?

_____

_____

_____

- What is my number one goal?

  _____

  _____

  _____

- How does this goal relate to my natural abilities?

  _____

  _____

  _____

- What problems do I want solved?

  _____

  _____

  _____

- What contribution do I want to make to the world?

  _____

  _____

  _____

To have control of your life, you need to have some kind of plan. You need to decide how you want to use your energies. You can get involved in many things and enjoy doing them, but to be effective with your time, you need to narrow it down to things you really want to do.

At all times, your plan should be flexible. When you are working with a plan, feel free to make changes, or revise as ideas come to you. If your goal can be accomplished sooner by altering your original plan, then alter it.

Remember, setting goals stimulates excitement, directs energy, motivates your efforts and delivers what you desire.

Just to Remind You...

Goals are vital to our psychological well being. Without them, we just live life as it comes along.

- The responsibility to determine what you want in life is yours alone.

- Eliminate "impossible" from your thoughts, words and beliefs, it's a failure word. Concentrate on why you can do something, not why you cannot.

- Identify what will fulfill you and then do it. Make a space for it in your life.

- *Tomorrow, next week, sometime, someday* are often synonymous with never. NOW is the word for success.

- When people look back over their life they regret actions and risks not taken far more than the mistakes they made (Cornell University study).

- We don't make time for anything when we are locked into a daily schedule.

- A goal is a purpose, a clearly defined objective.

- A goal stimulates excitement, directs energy, motivates our efforts and delivers results.

- Five Step Plan

  Desire

  Specific goals in writing

  A time frame

  Don't discuss your goal with others

  Visualize your goal.

- Anything that has been accomplished has first been created and imagined in your mind. First the vision, then the accomplishment.

- When we realize that our actions and feelings are the result of our own images and beliefs, we have the lever for change.

- We are successful when we identify ourselves with the reality of success, where we are at this moment. Rather than focusing on how far we need to go.

Chapter 7

"Forget mistakes. Forget failures.
Forget everything except what you're going
to do now and do it. Today is your lucky day."

– Will Durant, author and U.S. historian

It's Up to You

Have you ever told yourself that someday, when the time is right, you're going to do what you've always wanted to do? Unfortunately, for some of us, that day never comes. Only when circumstances force us to re-evaluate ourselves do we attempt to do what we've always wanted to do.

We also stand ready to give a host of excuses, reasons why we can't do it just *yet*. We complain about not knowing what we want to do. Or we make the decision that "the time isn't right," or "we are not as young as we used to be." If we were honest with ourselves, we would have to admit that we are not making decisions, but excuses such as:

"There's just not enough time for me to do it all."
"If only I could do what I want to do."
"I don't feel in control of my life."
"I will, when I lose weight."
"I keep getting interrupted."

"I'll get around to it when I have more time."
"It's tough to get organized. I have so much to do."
"I'm waiting till the time is right."
"I will when I have more money."

We just go on making excuses that prevent us from making use of the time we do have. We build a wall of protection around us with our excuses. When one dissolves, we find another to take its place. This is one of the reasons why so many of us are unhappy, frustrated, aimless and bored. Life is not interesting or fulfilling because we haven't committed ourselves to anything beyond our daily needs.

The more we deliberate about the best way to get started, the less likely we are to get started at all. We will not get anything accomplished unless we start it. We cannot start it until we make up our mind to start. We cannot make up our mind until we end our reluctance to start. It's a catch-22 situation.

It is this inability to make a decision as to what we want or what to do that keeps us from acting. To make any changes, to accomplish any task, we must come to a decision. Nothing happens until we do. We change and grow through action. It is vitally important to make a decision, but until we act, it remains a matter of "I would like to, but …." Excuses keep us from doing the things in life that we really would like to do.

Rudyard Kipling said, "We have forty million reasons for failure, but not a single excuse." Take a moment, and write down the answer to these three questions:

1. What are some of the excuses I use for not making changes?

2. What excuse do I make for not setting goals for myself?

3. What are some of the compromises I have made with myself?

It doesn't matter what kind of excuse we use. Just one can keep us from doing the thing we'd really like to do. When we have no specific plans for getting anywhere, we always have a lot of reasons to explain why we don't, why we can't, and why we haven't. When we are uncertain about a direction, we do nothing.

Trying to Please Everyone Is an Exercise in Futility

We all have had inspired moments when we see clearly how we can do certain things, but we don't believe in ourselves or in our ideas enough to make them a reality. Then sooner or later someone else comes along with no more ability or background and does the very thing we had envisioned for ourselves.

One of the main problems is our fear of criticism. Fear of criticism can bring on a lack of initiative, lack of ambition and an inferiority complex, because it creates a feeling of self-doubt. Fear of criticism is one of the most damaging emotions we can encounter in the pursuit of our dreams.

On the other hand, we feel comfortable when we have approval. It is one of our basic needs. It is through approval that we gain confidence and this strengthens our belief in ourselves. How many dreams perish because we don't get the needed approval?

The approval of others makes us feel good and seems to validate our decisions and abilities. We get caught up in pleasing because of our dependence on positive feedback.

Conversely, many people never set high goals because they are concerned about what friends and relatives will say. Unfortunately most people allow the continual input from others to affect them. When we repeatedly receive negative input, it is hard to keep from thinking, "Maybe I can't do it after all." When you start thinking that other people just may be right, you start making adjustments in your plans. The more people you talk to, the more adjustments you make.

It takes courage to break away from negative thinking of those around us. Entertainer and actor Bill Cosby had this to say, "I don't know the key to success, but I do know that the key to failure is trying to please everybody."

An enormous amount of talent is lost to the world for want of a little courage. When we have faith in ourselves, our abilities and talents, we can handle anything. As soon as we start doubting, we experience setbacks and encounter problems.

If Life's a Journey, How Come I'm not Moving?

The first requirement in business as in our social life is self-confidence in and the knowledge of who we are. The second one is initiative. Lots of people have ideas, but are reluctant to start a new venture. We want to be up and doing, but something seems to hold us back. If we are not aware of this, indecision can become habitual and prevent us from moving forward. The third requisite is the faith to go ahead and do things despite any obstacles. Inability to start may be due to timidity, doubt, resisting change, or past failures.

Successful people see an opportunity and seize upon it. The thought that they might fail doesn't occur to them nor does it influence their decision to proceed. They see the opportunity and know how to harness resources to help them achieve the best result.

The rest of us see the opportunity and wish we could take advantage of it. But we are fearful that our abilities or our money may not be equal to the task. While we hesitate, others who have the confidence in themselves achieve what could have been ours. Two things to keep in mind:

1. The only way to get rid of the fear of doing something is to go out and do it.

2. Not only are you going to experience fear whenever you are on unfamiliar territory, but so is everyone else.

A Risk Taker

Paulette Salo's career as an artist started very simply. She met a woman who needed someone to paint, decorate and sew for her. Paulette said she had a minor degree in interior design and got the job. In the following weeks, she made bedroom draperies and a bedspread. Her client then wanted her to paint a sailboat at sunset, between the swags over her bed. Without hesitation, Paulette said, "I can do that." While she had done no painting at all since she was ten, she just knew she could do it.

She bought the paint and brushes. She had no canvases. She did have pressed board, which she and her husband were using to put up a basement wall. Paulette cut out a piece the size she thought would fit between the draperies. She then found a picture of sailboats in a magazine about an inch and a half by one inch. She copied it in her client's colors. When she took the painting to her client, it was a hit. Paulette said, "She thought I was an artist. But I was just trying to make some money." Her client, still under the assumption that she was an artist, wanted her to paint a mural in her family room. She wanted a Paris street scene with bistros along a 15 ft wall. Again, without hesitation, Paulette said, "I can do that."

After her first job was finished, she thought that if she copied the paintings of the Masters, she could learn their colors, compositions and brush strokes. She got art books from the library and bought more pieces of pressed board and cut them to fit the inexpensive frames she bought at garage sales and thrift stores. She then started painting pictures to sell at mall shows, new apartment building openings and art shows on the city's streets.

Her next venture, several years later, was to open an art gallery in Buffalo, in a urban area near the metro. Paulette had her paintings and all her friends' paintings in the gallery.

When she planned the grand opening, her family and friends helped with the mailings. Her dad bought all the wine and her mother made cheese balls and cookies. With all the support from her family and friends, the grand opening was a huge success. By the end of the day, she had made more than three thousand dollars in sales.

Then her customers wanted their paintings framed. Paulette did not know how to do that. "I was so excited about the gallery opening, I didn't consider that people might want them framed," she said. On the following Monday she went to a framing store. She told the owner that she had all these orders to fill and that she did not know how to make frames. He said he would teach her how to do it. When she learned how to frame, she said, "I earned more money from framing than I did from the paintings."

With the success of her first art gallery, Paulette bought an art gallery in Minneapolis. After twelve years, she sold both art galleries. Her mother was terminally ill and Paulette stayed home and took care of her. Finally, at her mother's suggestion, she took a position at a local designer furniture store where she made many valuable contacts and learned much more about design.

It wasn't until after she was 60 that Paulette finally reached a point in her life where she realized that painting was really her true calling. It was then that she started painting her large murals in new homes, schools and offices. She painted a 15 ft. x 115 ft. mural at a metro shopping center, depicting the history of that suburb.

After that she then went into the faux-finishing business, working in homes around the city. She became so well known that she was asked to consult on a book for a publisher. After consulting on seventeen faux finishing books, Valspar Paint Company asked her to do the vignettes for a "how-to" book for their faux-finishing glazes.

Paulette still does faux finishing, as well as murals in private homes, but her favorite work today is painting angels. "My plans for the future," she says, "are to keep learning, to keep taking risks and to keep on painting, until I can't hold a brush."

You may have other decisions before you finally hear that "call for action." You may vacillate between one course and another. Or maybe you know instinctively what the right decision is, but you let others influence you.

It is those who are determined and persistent, regardless of difficulties, who achieve anything worthwhile in their lives. Ask yourself:

- Why is it difficult for me to come to a decision?
- Why is change difficult?

Playing It Safe

Fear is the number one enemy of success. Our ego's can be so delicate that we will refuse to seek winning just to avoid rejection or failure.. Many of us don't go into business for ourselves, or start something new, because we are afraid we might fail.

One of the healthiest attitudes you can develop is to be able to fail and look another person right in the eye, admit you failed, and know both the reasons why that failure occurred and what you're going to do to avoid the same mistake in the future.

In the past, most of us have failed in some undertaking. Our failures make us feel uncertain and insecure. We usually become more conscious of past failures when we are in the process of making decisions or working on a major goal.

In remembering our failures we are, in effect, reliving them and making them our present. If we are not sure of our abilities and ourselves, the resulting indecision drains our energy and dampens our enthusiasm. In such an environment we lose.

Whenever we do something new, we feel fear or discomfort. Even if we just think about a new action, we can feel the fear. Being uncomfortable is enough reason for us not to do something.

- Fear keeps us from asserting ourselves.
- Fear keeps us from being who we were meant to be.
- Fear prevents us from accomplishing our dreams.
- Fear drains our energy.

Fear also keeps us from taking the risks necessary for change. We develop a fearsome attitude about what we may encounter tomorrow, next month, or next year. We look out on the world with a jaundiced eye and the things we sense or anticipate are not good. This attitude takes all the joy out of living.

Sometimes we reach a point where we seem to be defeated and we give up when, with a little more persistence, we could have succeeded. Each time you feel like giving up, take a fresh look at what inspired you to set that goal in the first place.

Fear and faith are the greatest factors competing for control of our minds, especially when thinking in terms of setting or achieving goals. We have all had experiences that were hurtful or disappointing. These experiences can make us doubt our ability to succeed. It is the tendency to focus on the negative aspects of life that helps to impress them deeper in our mind.

Fear is a powerful force. It prevents us from getting what we want from life because it keeps us from taking risks. What are your fears? Are they the fear of:

- Asserting yourself?
- Changing careers?
- Being alone?
- Aging?
- Public speaking?

Everyone is afraid of something.   List your fears and write down what each fear prevents you from doing.

We have to face the fact. No philosophy will help us to achieve if we doubt our ability to do so. No matter how hard we work for success, if our thoughts are filled with the fear of failure, they will paralyze our efforts. You may find you did not achieve your original goal because:

- The timing wasn't right.
- You were working on someone else's goal.
- It was not where you wanted to put your energies.

Perhaps just re-thinking your goal can revive your motivation and determination and give you the inner strength to move forward again with renewed enthusiasm. You need to keep in mind that everything develops in its own time. What is one change you could make in your life right now that you've been avoiding, because it's scary or uncomfortable?

You don't have to apologize for anything – a slow start, a change of heart or a less-than-perfect performance. Sometimes it's not a matter of giving up, but of going in a new direction. Here are a few pointers to consider:

1. Don't try to prove anything to anyone regarding your decision.
2. Use your "failure" time to develop yourself.
3. Prepare for the time when another opportunity will present itself.

Self-Doubt

The surest way to attract failure is to picture its possibility. You cannot think success and failure at the same time. One or the other must dominate. An old, but valuable adage states, "A journey of a thousand miles begins with a single step." It's imperative that you discard thoughts of past failures and your fear of future failures. When you finally come to a decision, stay with it. Listening to others is one of the first don'ts when you are in the process of change. Don't discuss your decision to change, with anyone who has an inclination to resist change. Sounding out others for reassurance does not eliminate the fear of anxiety in making a decision. In fact, if you discuss important matters with just anyone, you may create more anxiety and confusion for yourself.

Other people may not be as enthusiastic about your ambition as you are and will give you twenty reasons why you shouldn't or can't do it...and if you're not careful, you'll think of twenty more.

We also make a mistake when we look to others for advice as to what we should or should not do. Why are we so willing to give others the label of "expert?" That is what we do each time we accept their solution, doubts and fears.

There is an old story of a man who sold hot dogs by the side of a well-traveled road. He couldn't see or hear too well so he had no radio and read no newspapers, but he sold good hot dogs.

He put up a sign about how good they were and how he used fine ingredients. People came from miles around to enjoy them. He increased his meat and bun orders and bought a bigger stove to take care of his trade. He even called his son home from college to help him.

When his son saw the large orders his father was placing, he cried, "Dad, haven't you been listening to the radio? There's a depression going on. The European situation is terrible and the domestic situation is even worse."

Whereupon the father thought that since his son had been to college and listened to the radio and read the newspapers, he ought to know. So the father cut down on his meat and bun orders, took down the sign and no longer bothered to stand on the side of the road selling his hot dogs. His sales fell almost overnight. "You're right," he said to his son, "we certainly are in the middle of a depression."

In every major decision you may be in conflict with yourself whether to act or not to act. If you are not aware of this, indecision can become habitual and prevent you from taking constructive steps. You can do several things to avoid the tendency to wait until conditions are just right before you act:

- Accept the possibility that there may be future obstacles and difficulties.
- Don't waste time beforehand worrying about those possibilities.
- When you have a problem, you always have two options: worry about it, or solve it.
- Find solutions to difficulties when you encounter them.
- Do something (no matter how simple,) that shows action.
- Write a letter or make a telephone call asking for information.
- Don't harbor doubts about the decision once it's made.
- Start each day with the conviction that many wonderful new ideas will come to you, that you are going to encounter new situations, which will provide unusual opportunities.

One of the negative habits we acquire over the years is worrying. At one of my seminars, I asked the question,

"What is the difference between thinking and worrying?" One woman said, "Worrying is what we do at night." Worrying is like rocking. You're moving but you're not getting anywhere. One study showed that, of all the things we worry about:

- 40% never happen
- 30% are in the past
- 12% are needless
- 10% are petty and small
- Only 8% are real and a legitimate worry

These worries can be divided into two groups: Those we can solve and those we cannot solve. In short, 92 percent of the things we worry about are unnecessary and time-consuming. Most of our problems usually fall into the solvable group.

The next time you have to make a decision, don't concern yourself with what someone else thinks or would do. Instead, make the decision quickly, according to how you feel inwardly and how it looks to you. If you do, your self-confidence will increase with each decision you make.

Here are four steps to help you avoid hesitation when making major decisions:

1. Trust your instincts. Don't harbor doubts about the decisions you have made.
2. Once you make a decision, don't waste time reviewing or rehashing it.
3. Meet problems and obstacles as they arise, not in your head beforehand.
4. Act promptly on your decision.

Take Charge

First make a decision to eliminate all the non-essential activities you have become involved with over the years. They fill up time and do nothing for you.

Any decision you make will not be firm until you do something about it. The longer you put off doing something, the shakier your decision becomes. Once you make a decision, don't waste time reviewing or rehashing it. Begin by trusting your own decisions. If you want to make a decision but you feel less than sure about the matter at hand, ask yourself:

- What do I want?
- What will I lose?
- Have I anything to gain?
- Should I stay where I am?

The only time a change in your life will have a maximum chance of success is after you have examined who you are, what you think you need, what you would like, and what is possible. Then come to a decision about it by yourself.

William James, the father of American psychology, suggests three steps to take when you finally make the decision that you really want to change:

- Start immediately.
- Start flamboyantly.
- Make no exceptions or excuses.

You only have one life to live. So, while there is still time, don't waste it making excuses or thinking you don't have what it takes. Staying young requires an optimistic, take-charge attitude that gives you a sense of control over your life. If you see yourself as in charge of your life and in control, you feel strong, capable and confident. Make the decision, "This is what I want, this is what I'll have." Decide, choose, dream and be positive.

It's Your Move
Write your thoughts on each of these questions.

• What are some of the excuses I use for not making changes?

_____

_____

_____

• Why is it difficult for me to come to a decision?

_____

_____

_____

- Why is change difficult for me?

_____

_____

_____

- What excuses do I make for not setting major goals for myself?

_____

_____

_____

- What are some of the compromises I have made with myself?

_____

_____

_____

There is always a risk with starting out again, in trying something new. Once you decide to change some area of your life, do something. Action strengthens your confidence. Without action, your thoughts become worrisome and your confidence is undermined.

While we know little about the why and how of our subconscious, we don't need to concern ourselves with how it works, but that it works. Ari Kiev, M.D. said, "Once you decide to act, you will discover an amazing source of power within you."

Remember, the first step in making a change is the decision to change, to decide what you want out of life.

Just to Remind You...

We always have lots of reasons to explain *why we didn't*, *why we can't* and *why we haven't*. When we are uncertain, we do nothing.

- Many times when we think we are giving reasons for not doing something, what we are doing is giving excuses.

- Nothing gets accomplished until we start something.

- Trying to please everybody is an exercise in futility.

- Fear of criticism is one of the most damaging emotions we can encounter in the pursuit of our dreams.

- The approval of others makes us feel good and seems to validate our decisions and abilities.

- When we have faith in ourselves, our abilities and talents, we can handle anything. As soon as we start doubting, we experience setbacks and encounter problems.

- Indecision drains our energy and dampens enthusiasm.

- Trust in your own decisions. Action strengthens confusion.

- The next time you have to make a decision, don't concern yourself with what someone else thinks or would do.

- Of all the things we worry about:
  40% never happen
  30% are in the past
  12% are needless
  10% are petty and small
  Only 8% are real and legitimate worries.

- When you have a problem, you always have two options: worry about it, or solve it.

- Once you decide to change some area of your life, do something about it. Action strengthens confidence.

- You only have one life to live. Don't waste it making excuses or thinking you don't have what it takes.

Chapter 8

"Success in life is a matter not so much
of talent or opportunity
as of concentration and perseverance."

– C. W. Wendte, author

Keep Focused

When my father was in his late eighties, and not able to get around well, he asked me to come to live with him in Neillsville, Wisconsin. He said, "I'm afraid of the winter coming on and of dying alone." After much thought, I said, "yes." Driving from Minneapolis, Minnesota to Neillsville, Wisconsin was like driving into an envelope. Neillsville was more than a hundred miles to an airport. But I knew, if I planned my time, I could still continue to pursue my own goals and do what I had to do for my dad. I had it all worked out in my own mind and on paper.

In the past, my dad had been a serious vegetable gardener and at one time he owned a small farm. But because of his health, he could no longer plant nor tend a garden. One day, early in the spring of my first year with him, he asked me if I would like to learn how to "make garden?" I thought I could handle a small garden, so I agreed.

Lessons Learned

He gave me a number to call, which I did, and the following Saturday, a farmer arrived with his rotor tiller. He used it to cut a 75 by 50 foot swath in the back yard, which to me looked as big as a football field! "Somebody has got to be kidding," was the only thing I could utter. "How can I possibly plant that entire garden, much less weed it?" My dad had a way of ignoring stupid questions. So there was my first lesson: "You do whatever it takes to get the job done."

While my dad stood by with his walker, watching me, I began planting three rows of potatoes, two rows of onions, two rows of carrots, four short rows of corn, tomatoes, peppers, lettuce, cucumbers, zucchini and garlic.

The carrots, onions and corn never came up. My dad was not pleased. He said "You planted them too deep!" The garlic never appeared. He said, "You probably planted them upside down!" The zucchini blew up like balloons each day, and daily the rabbits and I were in a heated race to see who would have lettuce for lunch. On a scale of one to ten, my first attempt at gardening drew a miserable four as far as my dad was concerned. I breathed a sigh of relief after harvest.

The following spring, my dad said: "Are we 'going to make garden' this year?" I said, "It's okay with me, if it isn't too big." However, neither one of us informed the farmer that we were planning on a smaller garden this year. Much to my chagrin, I ended up with the same size garden as the previous year: 75 by 50 feet.

I then left for Peoria, Illinois to speak to the American Business Women's Association. Leaving behind a standing ovation from these 650 women, I returned home. As I drove up to the house, a huge mound in the backyard greeted me. Luggage in hand, I went into the house. I said, "Dad, what's all that black dirt doing in the backyard?"

"That's not black dirt," he said, "that's manure."

He then gave me his action plan. I was to purchase a spade from the Farmer's Coop and buy 5 lbs. of onion sets and ten pounds of seed potatoes. I hadn't even unpacked from my trip. "I don't believe this is happening to me," is a phrase I was to repeat many times over in the days to come. The second lesson: "When you have the plan, you're in control."

The first thing I found out about manure is that you can't shovel it; it just clumps. My dad said, "Use the spade, that's what it's for." For the next solid week I dumped, spread and grumbled. To add to the agony, the wheel came off the wheelbarrow in the middle of the garden. More grumbling as I replaced the nut on the wheel and continued with my task.

Finally, on the last day, I got up early to increase my efforts twofold. I was not happy. Then I realized that all week I had been working on my father's goal. I decided to make his goal my goal. After spreading manure on the garden, I would give myself a reward. It worked. I had more energy and enthusiasm for getting the job done than I'd had the entire week since I started the project. Due to all the extra effort and manure, we had a beautiful garden that flourished all summer. The third lesson: "Satisfaction comes from achieving your own goals."

I turned 60 that summer and I knew that if I could plant

a 75 by 50 foot vegetable garden by myself, I could do just about anything I set my mind to. I might add that, 'learning how to make garden,' was a character building experience.

Time Is Life

Today, everything moves fast, or so it seems. Sometimes the pressures we're under are the result of trying to do too many things in too short a time. We find ourselves saying: "How can I possibly do everything I need to do today?" "The things I do aren't necessarily the things I want to do." "I'm too busy to get things done."

In establishing our goals, we set a course for our life, and determine what we will do each day to achieve our objective. Sometimes a goal will seem too far in the future. It seems that we will never achieve it, and we might fall back into our old habit of consuming time without purpose.

Some of us participate in activities or projects to please others even when we don't really want to. Until we learn to be selective in saying yes, and comfortable with saying no, we will not have the time or the energy to do what we want. Routine activities can prevent us from having priority time scheduled to pursue a major goal. It's important to have a plan for every day. If we don't write down what we want to do, we may end up working on someone else's plan.

The three qualities that separate people who *do* things, from people who merely think about doing them, are:

- Decision-making
- Concentration
- Persistence

Concentration is focusing all your attention on one objective and refusing to consider anything that is not pertinent to the objective. If we lack the power of concentration, there is always the possibility of getting involved in other time-consuming interests.

The extent of our power to concentrate is an acquired habit. To strengthen this ability, we need a deep interest in our objective. That is why it's important to have an action plan and to focus on top priorities. The more we focus on what we want, the stronger our desire becomes. We need to eliminate doubt when thinking about achieving our goal.

It is vitally important to concentrate on one goal at a time instead of scattering our efforts. Many of us shift from one activity to another without focus. When we extend ourselves into other activities, we weaken our power to achieve our objectives.

For life to have purpose it must be planned and directed, no matter what our stage of life. If we want to get somewhere, we have to know our destination. Planning is a vitally important first step in getting results, but it can never be a substitute for action.

When we have the urge to do something, we must act. Our intentions may be the best when we say we are *going to* do something, but *going to* can imply a future time, next week, next month or next year. We need to change the phrase, "I'm going to," to *now*!

The Power of Focus

Lee Boyan wrote a business book entitled, *Successful Cold-Call Selling*. He said, "The one important thing, when writing the book, was *focus*. The magic of focus is that it releases your creative juices."

His suggestion for anyone contemplating writing a book is "know in your heart of hearts that you are going to write this book no matter what. Accept no excuses from yourself. Don't ever allow yourself to think, 'I'm too tired today,' or 'I don't feel like it,' or 'I can't think of anything to write.' Just sit there with pen or pencil or at the keyboard. You will be surprised how ideas will flow because of your determination and focus. Trust in your creative ability. It's there."

Lee also shared an experience he had while writing his book. He said, "I just wrote what I thought was my best stuff and than ran out of ideas. I started to become discouraged." He then said to himself, "Lee, you are going to finish this book. You are going to sit here for at least two hours no matter what." Soon, he wrote a sentence. Then he wrote another sentence. Then he wrote a paragraph. Then he finished a page. Next thing he realized, he had come up with what was the best story in his book. It became the signature story in his speeches and seminars.

He went on to say, "it is important to realize that you are connected to a cosmic consciousness that holds a wealth of creative power. Believe in that – trust in that! It's there for you."

When you hold onto the belief in yourself and keep trying, you become receptive to the creative part of your mind, your possibilities and your next step. Your success is predictable when you:

- Write down each day the five or more important things you want to accomplish.

- Do something each day that pertains to your goal.
- Spend some time each day on positive affirmation and visualization.
- Forget about past mistakes.
- Persist in spite of obstacles.

Persistence

Former President Calvin Coolidge said, "Nothing in the world can take the place of persistence. Talent will not; nothing is more common than unsuccessful men with talent. Genius will not; unrewarded genius is almost a proverb. Persistence and determination alone are omnipotent."

Persistence enables you to return repeatedly to your central focus, renewing your inner strength despite opposition, failure, obstacles and doubt. If you have this quality, you will always win out.

Many of us have failed at certain things in our lives, but what difference does it make how many times we fail if, in the end, we achieve what we want? When you achieve your goals, failure is beside the point.

To simplify your life, you need to:

- Know what it is you really want.
- Decide what you have to do to get it.
- Make a plan.
- Plan your activities for each day.
- Do one thing at a time.
- Stay focused.

An intense interest in the activity is essential for concentration. When you focus on a project, you are oblivious to everything around you.

The realistic way to look at failure is to see it as a learning experience. Whether or not a person fails is not nearly as important as what happens after the failure. Do you quit or go on? When you fail, one of the healthiest attitudes you can develop is to admit that you failed, and know both the reason failure occurred and what you are going to do to avoid the same mistake in the future.

Personal Effectiveness

The major resource we all start out with is time: all the minutes, hours, days, months and years that we're alive. Time is our most precious element, and we cannot thoughtlessly let it slip away from us. In the writings from the Sanskrit, it says, "Look to this day for it is life, the very life of life. In its brief course lie all the varieties and realities of your existence."

Try to come up with new ways to help you get more control of your time. This list may help:

- Plan the most efficient way of completing a project. Decide how much time should be allotted.
- Are there responsibilities that could be done just as well by others?
- Focus your total concentration on the job at hand. If you try to do more than one thing at a time, you will dissipate your energy.

Regardless of how simple it may seem, begin moving toward your goal by making your next task a move in the right direction. The important thing is not where you were, or where you are, but where you want to be.

It's Your Move

Write your thoughts on each of these questions.

- What routine activities get in my way that prevent me from having priority time to pursue major goals? Explain how.

_____

_____

_____

- Do I get invovled in activities or projects to please others? Explain how.

_____

_____

_____

- Am I too busy to get things done? Explain how.

_____

_____

_____

- Do I get involved in things that aren't necessarily the things I want to do? Explain how.

_____

_____

_____

Focusing on your objective further reinforces it, reducing distraction and self-doubt. From time to time think about how you will feel when you achieve your goal. This will stimulate you to act, regardless of what feelings of inadequacy and frustration you may have. Thomas A. Edison said, "Many of life's failures are people who did not realize how close they were to success when they gave up."

Remember, focus on your abilities, talents and strengths. In this manner, you will be less stressed, more creative and assume control of your life.

Just to Remind You...

We all start out with the same amount of minutes in a day. It is what we do with them that counts.

- Planning is a vitally important first step in getting results, but it can never be a substitute for action.

- Some of us get involved in activities or projects to please others even when we don't really want to.

- The three qualities that separate people who do things, from people who merely think about doing them, are: decision-making, concentration and persistence.

- Concentration is focusing all your attentions on one objective and refusing to consider anything that is not pertinent to the objective.

- The more we focus on what we want, the stronger our desire becomes.

- Learn to say "yes" when you want to and say "no" when you need to, so you have the energy to work toward your own goals.

- When you hold onto the belief in yourself and keep trying, you become receptive to the creative part of your mind, your possibilities and your next step.

- Make every move you take in the right direction toward your goal.

- An intense interest in the activity is essential for concentration.

- Persistence enables you to return repeatedly to your central focus, renewing your inner strength despite opposition, failure, obstacles and doubt. If you have this quality, you will always win out.

- Try to come up with new ways to help you get more control of your time.

- Whether or not a person fails is not nearly as important as what happens after the failure. Do you quit or go on?

Chapter 9

"It is not only what we do,
but also what we do not do,
for which we are accountable."

– Jean-Baptiste Moliere,
French playwright

Life can be a Big Put Off

I learned many lessons from my house fire. The biggest was not to put things off. I had put off many things that would have gone unnoticed if the fire hadn't happened. Some had serious consequences, while others were minor.

As a speaker, I did a lot of traveling and stayed in many hotels that had one thing in common: white towels. I really enjoyed using those white towels. But then, I'd return home and all I had were old mismatched, colored towels. One day I decided to buy myself six white bath towels, six hand towels and six wash clothes. I brought them home and folded them up, putting the hand towels on a small shelf in the bathroom, and the bath towels and washcloths in the linen closet. Then guess what? I continued to use the old colored towels.

The following week my grandson Andy came to stay with me for a month. He was fifteen years old at the time. I decided to give him the rules of the house immediately. One of the rules was: "Please don't use any of my new white towels." He said, "it didn't matter to him."

About two weeks later, I walked into the bathroom and there hanging on a hook was one of my new bath towels limp and damp. I couldn't believe he had the nerve to disobey me and use a new white bath towel. I hadn't even used them! When he came home from school, I confronted him.

Now here's a kid who has been in school all day learning, dealing with teachers and other teenagers. He walks through the door and my first words were: "Andy, why would you use one of my new white towels? You had all the other colored towels to choose from." His answer was, "Grandma, a towel is a towel!"

I had grown up during the depression when the accepted belief was, "make do, do without, eat it up, and wear it out." I was not about to accept his philosophy.

One or two days later, we had the fire. To make a long story short, the fire destroyed the hand towels on the bathroom shelf. It destroyed all the towels in the linen closet. I had put off using those new white towels and now they were all gone. They were all gone except for the one that Andy used. That towel was still in the clothes hamper in the basement.

Many people play the game of "I'll be happy when I get my bills paid, when the report is finished, when the house is painted and when I get on top of things." Think for a moment. If you had six months to live, what would be the most important thing you would want to do, to finish and to leave behind?

- What would you change about yourself or your life now?
- What limits do you have now that you would want to look at differently?
- Would you have a more positive attitude toward each day you lived?
- Would you waste the hours that make up your life?
- How would you feel about today?

What's a Day Worth?

In assessing the work of Grandma Moses after she died at the age of one hundred and one, John E. Canady, author and critic, concluded that she was not a very great artist, according to the standard of excellence passed down through the centuries. But he noted that she had a very special talent. "Her magic was that she knew how magical it was to be alive, and in her records of her life, she managed to relay some of the magic to the rest of us."

In contrast, I overheard a conversation in an elevator one morning as a woman said to her companion, "Today seems like Monday." His reply was, "Every day seems like Monday to me."

How many of us find a Grandma Moses kind of magic in our lives? How many of us are excited about life this moment, rather than living in that nebulous time we call "someday," when we will have more money, more time, more love and more fun?

There is a legend about Aaron, a fisherman who lived on the banks of a river. Walking home one evening after a hard day's work, with eyes half closed, he was dreaming of what he would do when he became rich. Suddenly, his foot struck against a leather pouch filled with what seemed like small stones. He picked up the pouch absentmindedly and began throwing pebbles into the water.

"When I am rich," he said to himself as he threw a stone, "I'll have a large house." He threw another and thought, "I'll have servants and wine and rich food." This went on until only one stone was left. As Aaron held it in his hand, a ray of light caught it and made it sparkle. He suddenly realized that he held a valuable gem. He had been throwing away the real riches while he idly dreamed of unreal riches in the future.

Don't Put It Off

We could go through our entire lives thinking that just a few more weeks, months, or years will have to go by before we can enjoy ourselves – just as soon as the present problem is over. If we continue to put things off until tomorrow, we'll find still more things to do that will concern us.

Each of us starts with the richness that constitutes our very life. What we do with the precious gift is up to us. An Arabian Proverb states that: "Four things come not back, the spoken word, the sped arrow, the past life and the neglected opportunity."

Life seems to accelerate as we get older. The days seem shorter, and the list of promises to ourselves gets longer. One day we realize that all we have to show for our lives is a litany of "I'm going to," "I plan on," and "Someday, when things settle down a bit."

The things we will regret most of all in our lives, will be the things we put off, the dreams we let slip away, relationships we failed to nurture and projects we started but never finished. Ask yourself, "Am I actively living my life for the greatest enjoyment so that each day holds within it a chance to repair, rejuvenate, revitalize and start over?" Keep in mind that tomorrow isn't promised to anyone. Therefore:

- Do something you enjoy each day.
- Don't put off telling your family and friends how much you love them.
- Find the meaning in today.

It's important to have a philosophy of life that will help us relate to what time really is. Author Edna Ferber summed it up when she said, "Life is a fine thing. It's the finest thing in the world. Though hazardous, it's a unique thing, it only happens once in a lifetime." Sometimes we forget how precious life is, we are so busy living it, or just wasting it.

The only moment we can live is the present one. All past moments are gone forever and the future is just going to be another present moment.

A Personal Journal

In the book, *The Treasury of Quotes*, Jim Rohn said, "There are three things to leave behind: Your photographs, your library and your personal journal. These things are going to be more valuable to future generations than your furniture."

Many of us rarely put value on each and every day that we are alive, except perhaps when something special is happening, such as, a birthday, anniversary, graduation, or a family re-union. Otherwise, for most of us, days seem to run into each other.

Ask yourself: What separated today from yesterday? Was it the things you did, the experiences you had, or was it the thoughts you entertained as you went about your day? Nothing very exciting or memorable," you are likely to say.

It probably never occurred to you that someone, in years to come, might be very interested in what for you, was just another day.

So why don't you take a few moments, at the end of each day, to write about what you did, what you felt and what you hoped for.

Because your life is of value, think of someone who would treasure your words in the future. Why don't you decide now to dedicate your journal to a child who is very special to you, whether it's your granddaughter, grandson, your own child, or someone else. Think of what it would mean to leave that person a daily record of your life to read and cherished for years to come.

Taking hold of our present moment is one of the steps to living happily, not postponing our pleasures until "someday." We need to make a decision now to celebrate our life, then put into it love, learning, adventure and pleasure...whenever we can.

It's Your Move

Ask yourself: "What am I putting off?"

- List the things you are putting off at work, the project you meant to begin, suggestions you were going to make, the contacts you had meant to follow up.

_____

_____

_____

- Make a list of things you've been putting off around your home. What are some of the chores? Go through your house, room by room and write down all the things you have been meaning to do when you have more time.

_____

_____

_____

- What are you putting off in personal relationships?
  The phone calls you meant to make. The cards, letters,
  e-mail you wanted to send. The family reunions you
  wanted to organize. A friendship you'd like to renew.

  _____

  _____

  _____

- And finally, make a list of the things you've been
  meaning to do for yourself: the vacation you have
  postponed, the exercise class you wanted to start,
  the art class you wanted to take.

  _____

  _____

  _____

If we are not careful, we will not only put off the
unpleasant things, we will also put off the enjoyable things
in our lives. After author and columnist Erma Bombeck
learned that she had cancer, she wrote about the things she
wished she would have done and not put off. She said, "I
would have burned the little pink candle sculptured like a

rose, instead of having it melt in storage and I would never have bought anything just because it was practical, wouldn't show soil or was guaranteed to last a lifetime."

Remember, all the seconds, minutes, hours, days, weeks, months, and years we are alive become our lifetime. This is the most precious and priceless element at our disposal.

Just to Remind You...

If you only had six months to live, what would be the most important thing you would want to do, to finish and leave behind?

- How many of us get excited about life this moment, rather than living in that nebulous time we call "someday"

- If we continue to put things off until tomorrow, we'll find still more things to do that will concern us.

- Keep in mind that tomorrow isn't promised to anyone.

- The things we will regret most of all in our lives, will be the things we put off, the dreams we let slip away, relationships we failed to nurture and projects we started but never finished.

- Sometimes we forget how precious life is, we are so busy living it, or wasting it.

- Don't put off telling your family and friends how much you love them.

- Taking hold of our present moment is one of the steps to living happily, not postponing our pleasures until "someday."

- If we are not careful, we will not only put off the unpleasant things, we will also put off the enjoyable things in our lives.

- Life is the most precious and priceless element at our disposal.

Chapter 10

*"The journey into self
is not the most important journey,
it is the only journey."*

William Butler Yeats

Be Who You Are

On a bus trip downtown, I sat next to a nun from my parish. We chatted about children, school, religion and life. I said, "Sister, I think I know what hell is."

She flinched a bit, but seemed curious. I continued, "My idea of hell is that moment in time when we finally know, who we are, what we could have been, and what we could have done and it will be hell when we find out. I doubt whether she accept my philosophy, but it did give her something to think about.

I firmly believe that when we accept the fact that the power to do anything, be anything, and have anything, is within us, we will cease to be anxious or worried. Instead we will raise our ambitions high, knowing that we have within us the powerful resources to deal with life and all that it entails.

Every person is here to live life successfully in one way or another. We have all been given a purpose for our lives. But that's not all. We've also been given the talents to fulfill that purpose. We have been given our own identity, our own uniqueness. Never before has anyone appeared on the face of the earth with a combination of our qualities, abilities and talents.

To reposition ourselves, or find a new direction, we need to spend time alone in quiet contemplation. We need to find some unfamiliar environment to help break the connection with the routine aspects of our life, to gain a new perspective. Now is the time to ask ourselves:

- What haven't I done yet in my life?
- What opportunities are waiting for me?

Before any real change can take place in our lives, we must search within ourselves, become aware of who we are and what is possible. We will never know who we really are until we deal with the person we think we are.

There is a story of an old rabbi named Zuscha, who was asked on his deathbed, what he thought the Kingdom of God would be like. He replied, "I don't know, but one thing I do know. When I get there I am not going to be asked, 'Why weren't you Moses, or why weren't you David?' I am only going to be asked, 'Why weren't you Zuscha?' Why weren't you fully you?"

Among all the living things on this earth, human beings alone have the ability to consciously shape the time that lies between birth and death. We alone have the ability to decide what we will make of our lives and ourselves. We cannot afford to let society impose on us a lifestyle or life goals that do not correspond to our inner needs. Betty Friedan, author of *Feminine Mystique* and *The Fountain of Age* has a few positive suggestions:

- Cherish your choices and maintain control of your own life.
- Commit yourself to your passions in work and love.
- Risk being yourself, who you really are.
- Risk new things, risk new ways, risk failing.

Self-Evaluation

Throughout our life we undergo many changes. It seems that we are never able to stop and evaluate ourselves. Many of us never determine who we are and what we want to become at different stages of our lives.

In his book, *What Color is Your Parachute?* Richard Boles says that many people who are trying to decide on life changes have never taken an inventory of their experiences, nor listed in priority those accomplishments that made them the happiest and most fulfilled.

It is also important that we have an optimistic, *take-charge* attitude that will give us a sense of control over our lives. When we see ourselves in that position, we will feel strong, capable and confident.

The elements necessary for achieving success at any age:

- Know what you want.
- Have a plan.
- Stay focused and motivated.

- Find people to help you.
- Look like you are a success.
- Plan for future accomplishments.
- Never stop learning.

Living Her Dream

Today Judi Milton is a 57-year-old mental health nurse and an avid vegetable gardener. She would be the first one to say, "There is nothing special about me. I'm not particularly creative. I don't have any innate adventurous spirit that I can detect. Nothing about me seems to set me apart from my race. In my heart of hearts I believe this to be true."

Yet, in December of 1990, at age 43, she bought a trimaran sailboat and set out on a journey that was to last for five years. In that time she traveled twenty-five thousand miles, visiting eighteen foreign countries.

Judi's earliest and best memories are on water. She said, "My dad taught me how to sail. He lectured me relentlessly over the years until I learned the fundamentals. One summer, when I was 14 years old, he reached for his briefcase as he rushed out the door for his office and said, "Oh Judi, why don't you take the boat out. It looks like a nice day." I was stunned. I'd never thought to ask such a thing. Our sailboat was unique on the lake and not a toy. 'Antigua' was an eighteen-foot wooden keel boat built by hand, with an auxiliary engine. It was my father's pride and joy. It didn't take me long to grab a girlfriend. We spent the day sailing for the first time without dad's instruction and protection. At the end of the day I landed the boat under sail, at the dock, without incident."

"I knew, at that time," Judi said, "that I wanted to have a chance to sail as much as possible, as well as to do it in different places. What I said to people about sailing at the time was simply, "I want to see as much of the world as possible before I die. I want to sleep in my own bed at night while I'm seeing the world. I want to retire young and return to work when I'm older and need the insurance. I want to see and explore until it's not fun anymore or until the money runs out, whichever comes first."

That dream held her interest and kept her going while she worked, loved and raised her children in America. As a divorced mother of two boys, there was little time or energy left for more than a few passions. Sailing was one, and flamenco dancing was the other. Judi worked hard at balancing it all and dreamed of the day when she could indulge her passions. She said to herself "I should sail to Spain!"

While she kept the dream tucked neatly in her brain, time ticked away. One child had graduated high school and the other one would soon. Her house was all she had and she'd lived in it for seventeen years. It was falling down around her and eventually she realized she could no longer maintain it. Besides, she thought, a house would only hold her down. She put it on the market. Slowly it dawned on her that this could make everything possible. She started to think that she could now dream in earnest. She acted "as if" ocean cruising were the next logical step, even though she had absolutely no idea when, where, with whom, or how to bring it about.

Judi met Bill five days before she moved out of her house. She had rented a 16 yard dumpster and emptied it twice, throwing away a lifetime of accumulated stuff. Her two sons' outgrown cross-country skis were in her car. On her way to work, she stopped at a second-hand sports equipment store to sell them for the boys. She struck up a conversation with the store manager. She expressed an interest in used wet suits hanging on a rack. He asked why she needed them. She explained that she liked to sail her Laser (a one-person racing sailboat) and didn't want to wait until July to do it. Bill said he too, was a sailor. Within minutes, they realized that they shared the identical dream. She sold the skis, bought the wet suit and gave him her check (with her phone number printed on it).

"Sometimes," Judi said, "a dream will rush at you, double-daring you to make it a reality." She was comfortable with her own pace, harried though it was at the moment. Selling her house, renting another, moving, cleaning and working required every ounce of physical energy she possessed. She did not forget Bill, however. The day she moved from her house, she heard the phone ring from under the moving boxes. She said, "I knew before I answered the phone that it was him."

"We did some cursory dating," she said, "but it wasn't long before we began planning how to fulfill our mutual fantasy: to buy a boat and sail it wherever we pleased. We already knew we wanted to cruise on a trimaran. We thought what it meant to be living on a sailboat, eating, sleeping, cooking, doing laundry, dishes, housekeeping, writing, repairing chores, taking out the garbage, etc., all the while sailing upon a bumpy, rolling ocean."

"A trimaran," Judi says, "sails flat, unlike an ordinary yacht. A trimaran is also faster that a monohull. A trimaran has enormous wide decks to stroll on or to tend the sails in a storm. The trimaran will float, even if it is badly damaged. It's all repairable, leaving you with your boat and your life."

Judi's parents were planning a trip to California to visit her sister. While they were there, they found "Rapa," a trimaran that was moored in Benecia, California. They took pictures and made notes. Judi hired a California surveyor to inspect Rapa thoroughly. Then she hurriedly sent the owner earnest money to hold it until she could get there to sign the contracts. In the meantime she learned Morse code and radio theory at her father's insistence, so they could keep in touch by ham radio.

In June 1991, Judi and Bill packed up everything they would need, rented a U-Haul and drove to California to board Rapa. "We fell into the bunk, on the boat that now was our home," Judi said, "exhausted, triumphant and scared."

"What had we done? We'd sold or given away everything we had accumulated in forty-something years," she said. "We quit our jobs, relinquished our careers and forfeited any security we may have had for retirement. We'd left our families. We'd left the friendships we'd nurtured over the years. We had no idea what awaited us outside the entrance of the marina. We didn't have a telephone, a TV, an ironing board or a blender." And five months of hard labor lay ahead, getting the boat ready to sail.

Fourth of July. A marina on San Francisco Bay. The

weather was truly foul. Day after day cold winds made sanding or painting impossible. Judi dug for their parkas, their heaviest sweaters, and long underwear – the whole Minnesota-survival look. The choppy waves threatened to lift Rapa and set her on the dock. They were as miserable as they'd ever been in their lives.

"One day," she said, "Bill and I looked at each other desperately. Let's get the hell out of this godforsaken place." Judi made hasty plans to sail to San Diego, 600 miles south. She started calling marinas from a phone booth. Finally, she found a fine "Cruiser Special" price and a doublewide slip that Rapa required for her 22 1/2 feet width.

She said, "I did a little grocery shopping and then we sailed into the Bay of San Francisco, under the Golden Gate Bridge, and 60 miles out into the ocean we turned left."

At last they entered San Diego harbor. Already the air was warmer. "I peeled off more of my arctic wear until I found my shorts," Judi said. "The sun made my skin warm. Warmth – what a concept. It felt like a miracle. I knew we had done the right thing when, as we pulled into our slip, a dark-haired woman stood, smiling, expecting us, holding a large box of Dunkin' Donuts. We stepped onto the dock, tied Rapa securely, and introduced ourselves to Jenny, our next-door neighbor for the following five months of hard labor."

They worked constantly and bought a whole lot of expensive equipment. Judi's dad came to San Diego to work his electrical magic on the systems now aboard: radar, GPS, ham radio and its associated antennas, huge bank of batteries, a wind generator and miles of wire. "November approached," Judi said, "Bill and I were trying to feel our excitement about this 'dream-come-true,' but we were always pushing ourselves to exhaustion, trying to complete the projects so vital to the trip ahead. We postponed our departure date over and over again. There was always a critical repair or modification, always a gizmo we'd better buy for our safety or comfort or convenience, always something."

Then it dawned on them. They looked around the marina and thought about the wannabe cruisers they'd met. Many of them were still "getting ready to go" after years of never-ending projects and uncountable dollars spent on nautical gear. They talked the talk of going, but there they were, still at the dock. "You see," Judi said, "south of San Diego, a sailor runs right out of America, no more borrowing a nice car to run to one of the many boat supply stores; no convenient overnight delivery."

"Let's just go tomorrow, Bill," Judi said. "I'll bet no one ever feels ready to leave. The boat floats. Let's call it done and go." They looked at each other and at that moment they knew it was right.

Ever list-driven, however, Bill objected. "But we haven't got our provisions yet," he cried. "How can we leave without supplies laid in?"

"I've heard," Judi said, "they have food in Mexico." They laughed, stowed the tools, cleaned off the decks and went to bed, trying to clear their minds of objections to sailing away from the USA.

At dawn on November 12, 1991, they broke a "christening" champagne bottle across Rapa's bow. Jenny kissed them good-bye, then threw them the dock lines as they motored away from Chula Vista Marina. "I waved," Judi said, "until my arms were numb. Can there be a feeling like it in the world? Thirty years of dreaming, three years of planning and slaving and countless dollars spent, all toward this moment, for my dream."

Judi's travels took her south through Central America, through the Panama Canal, to the Caribbean and across the Atlantic to Spain. As she sees it: " My whole life up to the moment I left the dock in San Diego was merely the preparation for my original childhood dream."

They sailed away into the sunrise, through San Diego Harbor and out into the Pacific Ocean. Judi thought, "How many people at age forty-five can say truthfully, 'Life is an adventure, and it's all ahead of me?'

You are Your Own Power Source

We do many things in life that hold us back from being who we were born to be. It's never too late to make life enjoyable and meaningful. Anyone, whether single, married, divorced or widowed, can have a more joyful, productive and fulfilling life. It's up to you to decide. When you do, you'll be on your way to exciting changes that only you can bring about, changes that are necessary for your mental, emotional and spiritual well-being.

To achieve anything worthwhile in your life, you need to take a positive attitude toward yourself and toward what it is you want to achieve. Set aside some time, at least every six months, to decide where you're going. Find your priorities, ambitions and aspirations, not just in business, but also in the personal things. Take the risk of being who you are:

- Trust your own instincts.
- Stop measuring yourself against others.
- Have a strong belief in yourself.
- Live within your own set of values.
- Dare to follow your own inner guidance.

Everyone has been given a talent, and maybe you are already using yours. If not, what is the unique combination of traits and abilities you have? What occupies you naturally? This is where the clue lies.

The potential for achievement exists within all of us. To achieve our goals and find the success we desire, we must believe that we are our own power source. The three important points that will help us in pursuit of our dreams:

- Know and have confidence in our own talents and potential.
- Dare – attempt the seemingly impossible.
- Persist courageously in the face of all obstacles.

The only moment we can live is the present one. All past moments are gone forever and the future is just going to be another present moment.

Take the time to decide what you want your life to be in the next year or five years from now. Ask yourself: "What can I change inside myself and in my world now to make the dream possible?"

Start to create an abundant, meaningful and productive

life by living your life on your own terms, finding your passion and living your dream. The only moment we can live is the present one. All past moments are gone forever and the future is just going to be another present moment.

It's Your Move
Write down:

- What is unique about me?

_____

_____

_____

- What things do I like doing?

_____

_____

_____

- What things do I do best?

_____

_____

_____

- What is one thing I do naturally?

  _____

  _____

  _____

- What things would I like to start doing now?

  _____

  _____

  _____

- What things would I like to stop doing now?

  _____

  _____

  _____

- What things do I dislike doing?

  _____

  _____

  _____

- What things would I like to do well?

  _____

  _____

  _____

- Do I enjoy a fast pace?

  _____

  _____

  _____

- Am I comfortable with a slow pace?

  _____

  _____

  _____

- Do I like working with people?

  _____

  _____

  _____

- Do I like being my own boss?

_____

_____

_____

- What have others said I'm good at?

_____

_____

_____

- How will my change affect my lifestyle?

_____

_____

_____

- What field of endeavor has my education and experiences prepared me for?

_____

_____

_____

Each of us must go through the critical hour of facing ourselves squarely and declaring our own independence. At that time, we must accept all our faults and weaknesses, along with our strengths, courage and know how. This is our moment of true freedom.

Remember, it's up to us to take a realistic view of ourselves, to determine the possibilities that are ahead of us and to consider what action we need to take to ensure that our future will be productive, fulfilling, and above all – satisfying.

Ahead of us may stretch twenty, thirty or more years of possibilities and opportunities. We all have the freedom, if we wish, to reinvent ourselves and to release the powers of our creative minds, and, in so doing, to discover a new sense of purpose. What a gift: knowing you can always count on *that something* within you to give you new vitality, new exuberance and a new way of life.

Just to Remind You...

To achieve anything worthwhile in our lives, we need to take a positive attitude toward ourselves and toward what it is we want to achieve.

- We have all been given a purpose. We've also been given talents to fulfill that purpose.

- Before any real change can take place in our lives, we must search within ourselves, become aware of who we are and what is possible.

- We cannot afford to let society impose on us a lifestyle that does not correspond to our inner needs.

- Many of us never determine who we are and what we want to become at different stages of our lives.

- It is important that we have an optimistic, *take-charge* attitude that will give us a sense of control over our lives.

- We do many things in life that hold us back from being who we were born to be.

- Take the risk of being who you are.

- The potential for achievement exists within all of us.

- Take the time to decide what you want your life to be in the next year or five years from now.

- We all have the freedom to reinvent ourselves, to release the powers of our creative minds, and to discover a new sense of purpose.

What's age got to do with it?

In the final analysis, "What's age got to do with it"? Absolutely nothing! You can still, if you're so inclinded:

- Start a business

- Buy a condo

- Travel the world

- Write your life story and jazz it up

- Make new friends

- Volunteer

- Plant a garden

- Achieve success in some undertaking

- Have dreams

- Fail at something

- Believe in miracles

- Fall in love

- And, if you are so inclined, you can add to this list and send your thoughts to me.

Bibliography

Allen, James, As A Man Thinketh, Grosset & Dunlap, New York, 1927.

Boles, Richard, *What Color Is Your Parachute*, Ten Speed, California, 2004.

Bortz, Walter M., *Living Longer for Dummies*, Hungry Minds, New York, 2001.

Bronte, Linda, *The Longevity Factor*, Harper Perennial, New York, 1993.

Friedman, Betty, *The Fountain of Age*, Simon & Schuster, New York, 1993.

Givens, Charles, *Super Self, The Longevity Factor*,

Kingma, Daphne R., *A Garland of Love*, Red Wheel/Weiser, Boston, 1992.

Maltz, Maxwel, *Psycho Cybernetics*, Prentice-Hall, Inc., New Jersey, 1960.

Montague, Ashley, *Growing Young*, Bergin & Garvey, Massachusetts, 1989.

Olinekova, Gayle, *Power of Aging*, Thounder North Press New York, 1998.

Ullman, Samuel, *From the Summer of Years Four Score*, Fred S. Lang Co., Los Angeles, 1922.

About the Author

Joan Kennedy is a professional speaker and the author of *Don't Want Much From Life, I Want More!* and *How To Keep Your Staying Power!* She has also written a booklet entitled, *Everybody's Doing It!*

Joan also created a CD entitled, Lull-A-Baby, which is a collection of classic lullabies. After each lullaby, there is a loving affirmation to help instill a positive self-image for all listeners. Lull-A-Baby is also designed to help babies and young children fall asleep.

For two years Joan presented daily inspirational/motivational messages on an East Coast radio station.

Joan speaks to corporations, trade associations, colleges and universities, health care organizations, women's groups, senior and pre-retirement groups.

Joan delivers a timely message with content style and humor.

Joan's Talks and Seminars

Living Longer Staying Younger

What's age got to do with it?

Everybody's Doing It!

I Don't Want Much from Life, I Want More!

Contact Joan Kennedy for personal speaking engagements for your organization:

Joan Kennedy
3852 Raspberry Ridge Road N.W.
Prior Lake, MN 55372
952-226-3140
Email: JVKennedy1@aol.com
www.joankennedy.com

Order Form

Order additional copies of:

What's age got to do with it?
Send $14.95 per book plus $3 shipping & handling to:

Joan Kennedy
3852 Raspberry Ridge Road N.W.
Prior Lake, MN 55372
Phone: 952-226-3140
E-mail: JVKennedy1@aol.com
www.joankennedy.com

Attention corporations and organizations:

If you'd like to use *What's age got to do with it?*
for a fund raiser or premiums for your organization,
please contact
Joan Kennedy - 952-226-3140

Joan Kennedy's Lull-A-Baby
Positive loving thoughts
for your baby

Basic wholesome thoughts we'd all like to instill in our children to help them grow into confident, responsible happy adults.

Play the CD at naptime, playtime, after goodnight kiss time...anytime! The more your child hears it, the more it can help build your child's self-esteem.

- Tender loving positive affirmations created and recorded by Joan Kennedy.

- Enhanced by a collection of soothing, relaxing lullabies selected for their cheerful, comforting lyrics and melodies and sung by Peggy Mattola.

- Complete directions for use are included, along with all the positive phrases in print, so you may reinforce each affirmation at any time.